A STUDENT'S GUIDE TO SOCIALISM

HOW IT WILL TRASH YOUR LIVES

PAUL H. RUBIN

BOMBARDIER
BOOKS

A BOMBARDIER BOOKS BOOK
An Imprint of Post Hill Press
ISBN: 978-1-64293-671-1
ISBN (eBook): 978-1-64293-672-8

A Student's Guide to Socialism:
How It Will Trash Your Lives
© 2020 by Paul H. Rubin
All Rights Reserved

Cover Design by Cody Corcoran

Although every effort has been made to ensure that the personal and professional advice present within this book is useful and appropriate, the author and publisher do not assume and hereby disclaim any liability to any person, business, or organization choosing to employ the guidance offered in this book.

Post Hill Press
New York • Nashville
posthillpress.com

Published in the United States of America

Advance Praise for *A Student's Guide to Socialism*

"Most books on socialism show that it has always been a disaster. Paul Rubin takes a different tack: His wonderful book shows that socialism would be a disaster in the future for today's students. If the U.S. were to adopt socialism as advocated by Bernie Sanders, young people could expect their lives to be worse. They would be poorer, less free, and unhealthier. Besides, the gadgets they depend on (computers, smartphones, game machines, electronic readers) and the apps based on these machines have all been invented by capitalists, and future technology (artificial intelligence, 5G, biotech) would not be developed as robustly, if at all, in a socialist world. Every parent and grandparent of a student should buy a copy of this book."

—RAND PAUL, U. S. Senator and author of
The Case Against Socialism

"This is an important book. Today. And twenty-five years ago and twenty-five years from now. It exposes the lie of socialism: socialism is simply an alternative to liberty. Unlike liberty's other competitors—monarchy, theocracy, aristocrats, mob rule, or ethnic division—socialism has found allies in all centuries. Even our own. This Hydra-headed lie must be beaten back each and every generation. A King. An aristocracy. A central committee or a bureaucracy all serve themselves at the expense of the people. *A Student's Guide to Socialism* should be read by every student today and by their children and their children's children."

—GROVER NORQUIST, President, Americans for Tax Reform

"*A Student's Guide to Socialism* is a readable and powerful foray into what young people can expect for their future if the U.S. were to embrace socialism. Rubin is a master at explaining basic economic insights while avoiding technical jargon and math. Here, he uses accessible prose and relatable examples to show college-aged readers that socialism would reduce their lifetime income, their opportunities, and their freedoms."

—SUSAN E. DUDLEY, Director, The George Washington University
Regulatory Studies Center, Distinguished Professor of Practice,
Trachtenberg School of Public Policy and Public Administration

Also by Paul H. Rubin

The Capitalism Paradox:
How Cooperation Enables Free Market Competition

From Martie and Paul to our grandchildren:
Abby, Ben, Brian, Emily, Hannah, Mia, and Michael.

May you and all your contemporaries have an
even better life than members of our generation.

TABLE OF CONTENTS

PART II
IF YOU ARE STILL CURIOUS

INTRODUCTION

There are many books and articles on socialism. Why another? What can another book add to what we already know or can easily find out?

You can find discussions at any length and depth of analysis of the history of socialism; the effects of socialism on efficiency and inefficiency; the effects on equity, fairness, and income distribution. There is even a book dedicated to a discussion of the effect of socialism on the quality of beer. There are discussions of the Soviet Union, of Venezuela, and of the Scandinavian countries.

All of these analyses and discussions are backward looking—they describe the way socialism has worked (failed) in the past. They are at a theoretical or historical abstract level. The purpose of this book is different. It is written for students—mainly college students, although it is relevant for younger students as well—and for non-students. It is forward looking—How will socialism affect your lives *in the future*. You probably have only a vague knowledge of the Soviet Union, which collapsed in 1991, before you were born. Venezuela is in South America, and that part of the world always has government problems.

Scandinavia is a few frozen countries on the border of Europe. Efficiency, equity, fairness, and income distribution are abstract theoretical terms that don't mean much outside of class, if you take the right classes. Otherwise, they are just noise.

The purpose of this book is to explain exactly what socialism would mean for *you*, if it were to be adopted in the U.S. That is, I want to show exactly what it would mean for you, as a twenty-year-old student reading this book today, to live the rest of your life in a socialist country with a socialist economy. You live in a capitalist society, so you know something about that. But socialism is something you have never experienced. I want to get away from abstractions and explain exactly how socialism would affect the rest of your life. I have purposely made the book short so you will find it worth your time to read it. For the same reason, I have avoided jargon and most mathematics (which is hard to do for an economist) so you will find it readable.

The book is in two parts. Part I is the applied part—what do you actually need to know about what life would be like in the future under socialism. If you only read this part, the book will have fulfilled its purpose. Part II is more abstract, though still not too abstract. It provides some background on socialism—how has it actually worked in practice, why some people prefer socialism, how socialism compares with capitalism. If you are still curious after reading Part I, then Part II is for you.

Before beginning, I need a working definition of "Socialism." Just what am I talking about? There are lots of abstract and theoretical definitions. But I am not going to get into that, and I am not going to give my own definition. Rather, I am going to let the leading American socialist explain what he means. In a speech given on June 12, 2019, Bernie Sanders has defined socialism:

"We must take the next step forward and guarantee every man, woman and child in our country basic economic rights — the right to quality health care, the right to as much education as one needs to succeed in our society, the right to a decent job, the right to affordable housing, the right to a secure retirement and the right to live in a clean environment." Sounds good, doesn't it?

Actually, that is a mild definition of socialism, although, as we will see, even that version is enough to radically change the U.S. I will from time to time refer to the more standard definition, an economic system in which the government controls the means of production. An even more extreme version is the "Green New Deal," proposed by Alexandria Ocasio-Cortez (AOC), but this version is so extreme that it is unlikely to be adopted, and so it is not worth discussing.

Although the book is about socialism, I sometimes discuss communism. While there are many American advocates of socialism, there are few proponents of communism. Nonetheless, in their fundamental economic structure, the two systems are basically the same. Both systems are opposed to capitalism. Both systems advocate government ownership of the means of production and control by the "people," not by capitalist owners. Moreover, to many communists, and probably many socialists as well, socialism is only a step on the way to full communism. Additionally, socialism does not seem to be an equilibrium. Some socialist countries become capitalist and others move to full communism, but few stay in the middle. Therefore, we can gain some insight by considering socialism and communism together, as long as the distinction is kept clear.

This book is aimed at students, so the natural question that students always ask is, "Will this be on the exam?" You may view this book as a text for a course, Life 101. There is only one question on the exam: Will you support socialism? There is only one grade, and it is how you live the rest of your life. My hope is that after you read this book you will be able to make an informed judgement about whether you want a socialist or a capitalist future.

PART I

WHAT YOU NEED TO KNOW ABOUT SOCIALISM

CHAPTER 1

SOCIALISM, JOBS, AND INCOME

You are about twenty years old. With a normal retirement age of sixty-five, you have about forty-five years to work. You will probably spend about forty hours a week, about two thousand hours a year, on the job, whatever it is. Next to your family, your job is the most important aspect of your life. Your job and the job of your spouse will probably be your major source of income. Income in turn will determine important life decisions, such as where you live, where your kids go to school, what kind of car you drive, what kind of vacations you take, and when and where you retire.

SOCIALISM AND JOBS

What if we adopt some variant of socialism now? It is certain that it will take some time to fully adopt socialism. The U.S. is a big economy, and we cannot change its direction on a dime. Moreover, until we begin socializing the economy, we will not know exactly what will be socialized, which is why I referred to "some variant" of socialism. This process will create great uncertainty. Even the simplest variant—a public option for health insurance—will create uncertainty for business. A business will need to ask: How will this interact with the insurance I now provide for my workers? How much will it cost? How will it be financed? Will I have to pay more taxes for my employees? When Obamacare was being implemented, similar uncertainty and similar questions arose, and for that reason many firms were unwilling to hire new workers. An employer would not know the cost of a worker until those questions were answered and so would be afraid to hire. Similar questions arise for any other socialist project. For example, will Sanders's "right to a decent job" make it more difficult to lay off workers in rough times or to fire an employee who turns out to be incompetent? Because of this uncertainty, a firm will be more hesitant to add new employees.

One thing we know for certain is that economic uncertainty reduces investment and hiring. Thus, you, as a student now, will be seeking your first job in the teeth of a highly uncertain labor market. *You will not get a good job.* Firms will not in general be hiring for good jobs; they will hire a minimum number of workers for low-paying and easily replaceable jobs and will contract out as much work as they can. Bernie has promised "the right to a decent job" but, even if socialism fulfills this promise (itself doubtful), it will happen too slowly to affect your first job. (This is in addition to the tremendous shock to the labor market and the economy caused by the Chinese coronavirus.) Another thing we know for certain is that the quality of your first job follows you throughout your career. For example, pay raises are generally based on your current pay, and if you start off at a low pay rate, you will never catch up. Thus, you, as a member of the first generation hired into a socialist labor market, will pay a high price for this privilege. Your children could (but actually won't) benefit from Bernie's "right to a decent job" if it should happen, but you clearly will not. In attempting to create communism in the Soviet Union, Lenin and Stalin killed millions of people (see Chapter 11). They justified this by claiming that "You can't make an omelet without breaking eggs." You won't be killed in the movement to socialism, but you will be economically harmed—you will be an egg in the tasteless omelet the socialists are cooking.

Moreover, socialism will reduce your real, inflation-adjusted income. This is a simple fact—there is no way around it. There are several ways in which this will occur. Mainly taxes will be higher and wages lower than otherwise. Under socialism, government provides some goods and services that are otherwise provided by the market.

These must be paid for in some way, and that means increased taxes—whether income taxes, sales taxes, value added taxes, or the implicit tax of inflation. As a result of higher taxes, your take home real (inflation adjusted) pay will be reduced. Wages will also be reduced through lower productivity.

Why will taxes increase? Under Sanders's proposals, spending will increase by $97.5 trillion. Most of this is from Sanders's big three: health care, (Medicare for All) $30 to $40 trillion; climate, $16 trillion; and his jobs plan, $30 trillion. The rest of the increase will come from "small" increases, like $3 trillion on free college tuition and paying off all student loans. Bernie's plans would more than double the size of the federal government. Even including the plans for increasing revenue, which come to about $23 trillion, the remainder is 34 percent of gross domestic product (GDP), or $66,000 per family. (This paragraph is from Brian Riedl, 2019, cited in references.)

PRODUCTIVITY

The reduced income caused by increased costs for government services (discussed later) and reduced incentive to work caused by the increased taxes to pay for these services will reduce incentives to invest in both "human capital" (education, training) and physical capital, such as buildings and machines. It will also reduce the incentive to invest in research and development (R&D)—new technology. Productivity—output per hour per worker—grows if capital and technology grow. The reduction in productivity will occur because higher taxes reduce the return for investment and so there will be less investment. It is estimated that government spending would increase to 70 percent of GDP, and payroll taxes would increase from 15.3 percent of earnings to 27.2 percent. Reductions in capital investment and in R&D mean that productivity will grow more slowly, if at all.

There will also be reductions in incentives to use resources (capital and labor) correctly. This is because in a socialist system, prices will not allocate resources efficiently. In a capitalist system, our old friends supply and demand lead to an efficient use of resources—that is, supply equals demand, and there are generally no shortages or surpluses. In a socialist system, prices are arbitrarily chosen by the central planning organization, and there are commonly surpluses (resources wasted by producing too much of some good) or shortages (consumers do not get enough of goods they are willing to pay for). I discuss some examples later in the book.

Why should you care about productivity? Because growth in wages and earning ultimately depends on growth in productivity—the amount produced by labor and capital. In the U.S. we are used to real wages (wages above inflation) going up annually. This is because productivity increases. If workers do not in some sense become more productive, their real incomes cannot increase, because there is no money available to increase their wages.

So socialism will reduce productivity growth. What does that mean for you? Remember that you will function in the economy for about forty-five years—a long time. So we do not want to only consider the effects of policies on the next year or two; we want to have a long-term perspective because as a young person, you will live and work in the economy for a long time. Increases in productivity have a long time to operate. From 1974 to 2019, a forty-five-year period, real incomes per year for each person (that is, incomes over and above inflation) increased from $26,000 to $57,500. This represents an annual rate of growth of about 1.788 percent per year. (Actually, real—after inflation—incomes grew faster than this, but because we overestimate the rate of inflation, we also underestimate real income growth.)

With the same rate of growth for the next forty-five years (your working horizon), average income will grow from $57,500 to about $127,000. This increase of $70,000 is a real increase in income, just as the increase from 1974 to 2019 of $30,000 was a real increase in income, over and above inflation. That increase means that we now have larger houses, better cars, longer and more enjoyable vacations, better health and longer lives, better meals and clothes, earlier possible retirement, and better lives during retirement. (If you ask your parents or grandparents, they will be glad to tell you how much easier you have life.) Similarly, if your income increases by another $70,000 over the next forty-five years, you will have even more enjoyable lives, in traditional ways (houses, cars, retirement, and so on) and in ways that we cannot now even imagine. (Of course, part of the increase in our life satisfaction is due to technological improvements and new technologies, but those in turn depend on investment in R&D, which is also fueled by increased incomes. The mismeasurement of the value of such goods is part of the error in measuring inflation.)

Socialism will reduce the rate of growth of income. A possible estimate is that it will reduce the growth rate from 1.78 to 1 percent per year, which seems like a small change. (Actually, it will probably reduce it by more than that. Also, as we see later, socialism will reduce the base from which income is growing by increasing costs of medical care and increasing taxes. But we will ignore that for now.) If the rate of growth is reduced to 1 percent per year, then real incomes over the next forty-five years would increase to $89,000, an increase of $32,000 instead of the increase of $70,000 to $127,000, a normal increase in a capitalist market economy. We must also understand that the decrease in income is not all at once; each year incomes will be smaller with an increase of 1 percent per year than with an increase of 1.78 percent per year. That is, *every year* of your working life you will be poorer under socialism than under capitalism, and by the end you will be much poorer.

I don't want to quibble over the numbers. I have actually chosen them to be favorable towards socialism. I have ignored the decrease in income from shifting to a Medicare for All system, as discussed later. The 1.78 percent growth is historically true, but still somewhat low; in recent years we have seen growth rates of about 3 percent. The reduction in growth rates under socialism is probably larger than the rate I have used. But the basic point goes through: the effects of a shift in growth rates under socialism will be much greater for you as a young person than for me as an old person, or for Bernie Sanders, because Bernie and I have only a few years left to feel the effects of the reduced growth rate, while you have an entire working lifetime to suffer the consequences.

The important point is the rate of growth with compound interest. These rates are remarkably high. Since you have a long time for growth to accrue, the effect on your lifetime income of a small difference in rates of growth is quite large.

To better understand growth rates, look at the little table below:

Table 1: Growth and Income: Effect of Alternative Growth Rates on $50,000 in Forty-Five Years

1 percent growth rate	$78,500
2 percent growth rate	$122,000
3 percent growth rate	$189,000

Source: Computed by author.

What this table tells us is that if the average income today is $50,000 and if income grows at a 1 percent rate, then in forty-five years average income will be $78,000; if incomes grow at a 3 percent rate, then in forty-five years average income will be $189,000. Remember that these are real growth rates, growth rates over and above inflation. So even if a shift from capitalism to socialism has only a small effect on growth rates, it will have a very large effect on your income over your working life.

It might be suggested that any additional costs can be financed by taxes on the rich. However, the rich are already paying more taxes than the less wealthy. The highest-earning 1 percent of the population earned about 20 percent of income but paid 37 percent of all taxes under our current system. More could be taxed, but we quickly run into incentive effects as the richest (and most productive) citizens might retire earlier, leave the country, or invest in more certain but lower return opportunities. The rich can also shift the type of earnings to less taxed forms, such as capital gains. While there are proposals for a tax on wealth instead of income, such a tax is unconstitutional and would require a constitutional amendment, as did the income tax (the Sixteenth Amendment). From an economic standpoint, it is very difficult if not impossible to measure wealth and possible to hide or move wealth, so there is not much chance for this tax to be passed or to raise much revenue if it is passed. When a wealthy individual whose estate is subject to inheritance taxes dies, it can take years and thousands of dollars of accountants' and lawyers' time to value the estate. Under a wealth tax, we would perform such an evaluation every year. It is not clear how much revenue the government would get, but lawyers and accountants would get a lot, and hopefully there would be a little left for economists. Several countries have tried a wealth tax, but most have eliminated it because of the difficulty of measurement and enforcement.

Some additional spending can be financed by additional taxes on the rich, but the levels of spending proposed by the current socialists can only be financed by greatly increased taxes on the middle class.

TAXATION AND COERCION

There is another point about taxation which will become more important as our story continues. Taxation is fundamentally based on coercion. We pay our taxes because if we don't, dudes with guns will show up and arrest us. (Of course, most of us pay our taxes voluntarily, but deep down we know about the dudes with guns.) Once the government has our money, within limits it can do whatever it wants with it. For example, it can give it to those whom it favors (cronies) or those who help it get elected, if it has free elections. If not, it can support the police and military who keep it in power.

So incomes will grow more slowly under socialism. Over a forty-five-year life, even a small difference in growth rates will lead to a much smaller income and wealth. Taxes will also be higher under socialism.

CHAPTER 2

SOCIALISM AND FREEDOM

The most important distinction in society is between freedom and coercion. Free societies are run from the bottom up, based on individual decisions; coercive societies are run from the top down. In coercive societies, the state exists for the benefit of the ruler. In free societies, the state exists to benefit the people (or, more accurately, the state exists to enable the people to achieve goals that they cannot achieve individually, such as cleaning the air and water, providing defense, and public health).

The most important source of coercion is government. Historically, most governments have been coercive—dictators, kings, emperors, monarchs, rulers, sovereigns, czars, and sultans all wielded power and reduced or eliminated freedom of subjects. The most important source of freedom has been the free market. The free market allows people to control their own lives. Voluntary free exchange allows people to willingly trade on terms that both parties find advantageous. As we move towards socialism and replace free markets with government power, we reduce freedom. Much of the U.S. Constitution and the Bill of Rights (the first ten amendments to the Constitution) are aimed at restricting the power of government in order to maintain freedom. It is my belief that we in the U.S. have already gone too far in granting government excessive power, but even if you think that we are now correctly governed, you might be concerned about a massive shift of power to the government.

A movement towards socialism will greatly accelerate this increase in government power. Many countries have gone from democracies to dictatorships: Germany (Hitler), France (Napoleon), Venezuela (Chávez), Argentina (Perón), Turkey (Erdoğan), Italy (Mussolini). In many of these cases, the dictator was first elected and then increased his (all were men) power until becoming a dictator. This is sometimes characterized as "One person, one vote, one time."

The actual functioning of a dictatorship gives much power to bureaucrats. Laws are passed, which are ambiguous. Then the bureaucrats who enforce these laws have substantial amounts of power. For example, I worked as a senior economist, a bureaucrat, at the Federal Trade Commission. Our job was to police "deceptive" or "false and misleading" advertising. But all these terms are ambiguous. Because of this ambiguity, the economists and lawyers were able to disagree about whether some advertisement was deceptive. This ambiguity means that the bureaucrats had considerable discretion in deciding which ads to attack. The law is full of ambiguous terms (some examples: good faith, reasonable, excessive), which gives bureaucrats power in that they interpret these terms. If we expand the power of government (as would socialism, by definition), there will be more options for government bureaucrats to control our lives.

The United States Constitution begins "We the people of the United States...." This is a statement that the government of the U.S. comes from the people—it is a "bottom up" government. Power comes from the people, and other parts of the Constitution are aimed at enforcing this power and limiting the power of the government. This is the system of "checks and balances" that limits the power of any one part of the government. There are also clauses in the Constitution that enforce principles of free markets, including free trade between the states:

> Article 1, Section 9, Clause 5: No Tax or Duty shall be laid on Articles exported from any State.

> Article 1, Section 9, Clause 6: No Preference shall be given by any Regulation of Commerce or Revenue to the Ports of one State over those of another: nor shall Vessels bound to, or from, one State, be obliged to enter, clear, or pay Duties in another.

Article 1, Section 10, Clause 1: No State ... pass any ... Law impairing the Obligation of Contracts. [This one is mostly gone.]

Amendment 5: No person ... shall be deprived of life, liberty or property, without due process of law; nor shall private property be taken for public use, without just compensation.

The Fifth Amendment is especially inconsistent with socialism since it regulates the way in which the state can take private property, but under socialism there may be virtually no private property. Alternatively, the Fifth Amendment, if it is enforced, may make it impossible to have a true socialist government in the United States since this amendment requires that compensation be paid for any property taken for public use, and under socialism virtually all property might be taken, and so compensation would be impossible.

Under socialism, the government owns the means of production. This means that our bottom up government would be replaced by a top down government. If the government owns the means of production, then the government controls the economy and the society, and so has virtually any power that it wants. Moving to socialism would be the biggest change in the U.S. government in history.

Socialism necessarily reduces freedom. This is because socialism at a minimum forces us to pay for something we may not want through taxes. Taxes reduce our ability to spend our money as we want, and so reduce our economic freedom. To most people, economic freedom—the freedom to engage in voluntary transactions—is a very important component of freedom. Taxes reduce that freedom. Taxes are necessarily coercive. If you don't pay your taxes, a person with a gun will come and arrest you. Because socialism replaces voluntary transactions with coerced transactions, it necessarily reduces freedom.

As a familiar example, consider the public school system. We all pay taxes for public schools. Some choose to send their children to private or religious schools, which is allowed, but they must still pay the taxes for public schools. Public schools themselves are associated with a lot of government control. For example, all schools in a state must generally use the same textbooks. Schools commonly indoctrinate kids in whatever doctrine is fashionable or was fashionable when the teachers attended education schools. (When you were in school, did you learn anything about the controversies regarding global warming and its remedies? About the costs and benefits of recycling? About the downsides of government regulation? About the Second Amendment, regarding gun ownership?) The creation of charter schools and vouchers has actually increased freedom in this sector. (I am not advocating for or against public schools, merely pointing out that they reduce freedom. I am myself a big fan of vouchers and charter schools.)

Socialism can go beyond this. One proposed socialized medical system, Medicare for All, would eliminate all alternative sources of health insurance. In this case, not only would we be forced to pay for medical insurance for everyone, but we would be forced to purchase the government plan. This would be a serious reduction in our freedom. The previous effort to control medical care, Obamacare, allowed competition in medical plans but required all plans to have certain provisions. (Recall Obama's false statement, "If you like your plan you can keep your plan.") Under the "individual mandate" (now repealed) everyone was forced to either purchase a plan or pay a penalty for not doing so. This was also a serious reduction in freedom. Since medical care is about 16 percent of GDP, a government takeover of the medical system would be a significant move towards socialism.

An apparently less coercive medical reform would be the "public option"—a voluntary plan available to anyone who did not want or have access to a private plan. However, recent estimates by economists at the Hoover Institution have suggested that this program would either lead to massive tax increases or massive increases in the federal deficit. These tax increases would be too large to be paid by the wealthy; they would require tax increases for the middle class as well. They would also lead to longer wait times and lower quality of health care.

You might feel that markets coerce you as much as government: you must be on Facebook or Instagram to converse with your buddies, you need a cell phone to call your mom, your profs require that you use a computer to write your papers. But there are fundamental differences between government and markets. This is choice versus coercion: markets cannot force you to do anything. You have a choice about the type of computer or cell phone you buy. If you don't buy a cell phone, no one will put you in jail. If you don't pay your taxes, someone will. Socialism puts government in charge of more things, and so increases the range of coercion. This reduces freedom.

You might feel that since government makes decisions democratically, there is no coercion. But this is not true. Even though decisions are made by a majority, you must still obey them, even if you are in the minority. For example, in the market, if you want to buy a car, you can buy whatever brand is for sale and that you can afford. No one but you is involved in this decision. But if 51 percent of the citizens in your jurisdiction decide to build a road, you must pay your share, even if you hate the road and it spoils your view.

Another difficulty with government decisions is that they are lumpy. When you vote for a particular candidate or party, you are voting for everything that that party represents. It will never be the case that any party exactly matches your preferences, so any vote is a compromise. In a market, you can buy whatever exact menu of products and services that you might want. Think of a modern American drugstore or grocery store. Each of them offers a huge variety of products, and it would be difficult to desire something that is not available. If you do desire such a product, write a manufacturer, and if enough people agree with you, it will soon be available.

We must make some decisions collectively, but as we make more decisions collectively, freedom is reduced and coercion increases, even if decisions are made democratically. The way to maintain freedom is to make as many decisions as possible privately. Socialism does the opposite: it moves decisions that are now private into the public sphere, and so reduces freedom.

One very important freedom is freedom of the press. In the U.S. this right is protected by the First Amendment to the U.S. Constitution, the first right in the Bill of Rights: "Congress shall make no law ... abridging the freedom of speech, or of the press..." This right is important because without a free press, people will have no way of understanding what government is doing. Moreover, without this right, opponents of the government will have no way to explain their position and communicate with supporters.

All governments dislike a free press because the job of the press is to find errors and mistakes and point them out to the citizens. Fortunately, the First Amendment in the U.S. provides a lot of protection for the press, and the government is not able to suppress the press. Other countries do not have such protections, including other free countries such as Canada and England. Suppression of free speech is particularly important in socialist countries because socialism leads to poor economic performance, and governments want to conceal this by concealing how well other countries are doing in comparison. For example, China censors the internet. Information is totally controlled in North Korea. Access to books and magazines was severely limited in the Soviet Union. This limit also makes organizing to oppose government much more difficult since people cannot organize protests. In the U.S., these rights are protected by the First Amendment, which guarantees "the right of the people peaceably to assemble, and to petition the Government for a redress of grievances." (Some think that the Second Amendment, "the right of the people to keep and bear arms," is a further ultimate protection of the people from government.)

Socialist countries differ in their policies with respect to speech. Those that allow free speech sooner or later cease to be socialist. Those that do not, such as China and North Korea, remain socialist. The U.S. with its strong tradition of free speech would probably continue to have a free press, and so we might hope that if it should become socialist, it would be a temporary position. But Venezuela had a free press, and Chavez and Maduro have suppressed any opposition and have shut down opposing newspapers.

Even if speech is unregulated, socialism tends to suppress freedom. Return to the example of medical care. If the government has a monopoly on medical care, then any medical provider (doctor, nurse, technician) who loses his/her government job cannot find another job using his/her skills. Since people in the medical system are the most likely to learn about its faults, it becomes difficult for reporters, even if they themselves are not restrained, to learn about flaws in the system because employees do not want to risk their jobs by pointing out weaknesses. As socialism spreads, this problem becomes more pervasive.

Higher taxes under socialism also retard freedom. Taxes are a reduction in freedom and are ultimately collected by the ability of the government to use force. As taxes, and particularly taxes on the wealthy, increase, people have less money available to fund anti-government causes or to campaign for office themselves (as did Trump, Bloomberg, and Steyer). As tax codes and other laws become longer and more complex, it becomes easier for a malevolent government to find some law that an opponent has broken and to punish the individual. (Stalin: "Show me the man and I'll show you the crime." Folk saying: "A prosecutor can indict a ham sandwich.") As more and more sectors come under government control, there are more restrictions and more laws to break, and again these can be used to punish enemies of the regime.

Let us consider some of Senator Sander's "rights":

"THE RIGHT TO AS MUCH EDUCATION AS ONE NEEDS TO SUCCEED IN OUR SOCIETY"

If government involves itself even more than currently in the education system, we can be sure that its message will be pro-government. Even now government controls much of what is taught in our schools and universities, in part through its threat of denying grants to schools that do not toe the government line. If you are a college student, you are aware that you have hidden some beliefs in the name of not being penalized as being racist, or homophobic, or Islamophobic, or some other harmful -ist or -ic. You may be sure that at least some of your professors have also concealed at least some of their views. But if government increased its control over education, this censorship and loss of freedom would only increase.

"THE RIGHT TO A DECENT JOB"

It is not clear what this means. But if it means that the government would be the employer of last resort (that is, would hire you if no one else would), then again there would be a cadre of people dependent on the government for support, and therefore unwilling to criticize the government. And of course taxes would be used to pay their salaries, thus reducing the freedom of taxpayers. An alternative possible meaning is that employers would be forbidden from firing workers. This would add rigidity to the economy and make growth and creation of new products much more difficult.

PATERNALISM

Even well-meaning socialism can lead to paternalism—controlling you "for your own good." "Paternalism" means that the state is acting like a parent. As you grow up, your parents gradually allow you more freedom, until you are independent of their control. If you are a typical college student, you have recently escaped control by your parents. Why would you want to move from freedom from parents to being controlled by the state?

Even free governments engage in paternalism. Some examples include: Mayor Bloomberg of New York limited the size of certain soft drinks to reduce obesity. Many governments have limited interest rates that consumers are allowed to pay. Governments have limited use of certain drugs, such as marijuana. Governments have limited your ability to gamble. Governments have also limited or eliminated free exchange of money for sex to protect sex workers. However, in a free economy, the limit to paternalism is that voters can change the rules, as is now happening with marijuana which is rapidly becoming legalized. In a socialist state, since the state controls production, it is much easier to behave paternalistically.

OTHER RESTRICTIONS

So socialism would clearly reduce your economic rights—your right to spend your money as you please. Depending on the form it would take, it could also reduce other rights, such as your right to choose your own medical care. If carried to its logical extreme, socialism could reduce your right to speak or hear certain speech and could lead to dictatorship, as it has many times.

Besides taxes, socialism reduces economic freedom in other ways, on both sides of the market. On the supply side, if some industry is socialized, then workers in that industry must work for the government. It becomes impossible to seek a new employer if you do not like your current boss because there is only one employer. The ability to create new firms or new ways of doing business is eliminated.

Socialism also controls the demand side of the market. A consumer can only buy the products that the government decides to sell. If the Minister of Breakfast Cereal decides that children should only eat healthy cereal, then Fruit Loops, Frosted Flakes, and Cap'n Crunch are gone. If the Commissar of Autos decides that all cars must get at least forty-five miles per gallon and go no faster than fifty miles per hour, then many of our favorites are out. I worked for the Consumer Product Safety Commission, and I can tell you that if they could have, many of my colleagues would have banned many potentially (but not actually) dangerous products.

A humorous example of this is from the 1984 movie, *Moscow on the Hudson*, with Robin Williams. After leaving Russia and moving to the U.S., he is searching for coffee in a grocery store and becomes overwhelmed by the variety of coffees available, since little if any variety was available in the Soviet Union. Finally, he becomes disoriented and passes out. This episode is available on YouTube as "Coffee, coffee, coffee." The movie also provides a nice illustration of life under socialism.

One of the great advances of humankind is the movement from control to individual freedom. Such freedom is only available in a capitalist economy. It is astounding that so many want to move back to a controlled system.

ECONOMIC FREEDOM OF THE WORLD

Every year, the Fraser Institute (in Canada) and the Cato Institute (in the U.S.) jointly publish the "Economic Freedom of the World Annual Report." This index[1] is based on five factors:

- size of government: expenditures, taxes, and enterprises;

- legal structure and security of property rights;

- access to sound money;

---

1. Wikipedia. 2020. "List of Countries by Economic Freedom," March 23, 2020, https://en.wikipedia.org/wiki/List_of_countries_by_economic_freedom#cite_note-4.

- freedom to trade internationally; and

- regulation of credit, labor, and business.

As you would expect, the socialist countries are significantly less free than market economies. The first clearly socialist economy is China at 100th (and even then China is only partly socialist). Some of the countries I identify as formerly partly socialist are now very free—United Kingdom, 7th freest in the world; Denmark 14th; Sweden, 19th; Finland, 20th; Norway, 26th; Israel, 27th. Also note that the Nordic countries which have sometimes been identified as "socialist" are in fact quite free. The least free countries are those which we have identified as the examples of purest socialism: Cuba, Venezuela, and North Korea.

There are some interesting characteristics of free versus unfree countries. Free countries are richer than less free countries. In 2014, nations in the top 25 percent of freedom had a per capita GDP of $41,228 compared with $5,471 for the lowest 25 percent. Even the poor did better in the freer countries: the average income of the poorest 10 percent of the people in the freest countries was twice the average income of everyone in the least free nations. Life expectancy was eighty years in the freest countries, compared with sixty-four years in the least free 25 percent. Finally, even though this is an index of economic freedom, the most free countries had significantly more political and civil liberties as well.

SOCIALISM AND GOVERNMENT CHANGE

A very important component part of freedom is the right to change the government. There are several methods of changing governments. The simplest and most efficient is voting. While there are problems with voting, in the long run voting errors are more or less self-correcting as long as the right to vote is preserved. Truly socialist countries such as the Soviet Union, China, Cuba, and Venezuela generally do not allow voting, unless they allow some perverted form where the current government always wins. But consider several countries which at one time had large government sectors and eventually voted for much smaller sectors: the Nordic countries, Israel, India, and Britain. In Sweden, for example, tax rates increased radically in the 1920s and remained high until about 1990, when they were greatly reduced. Tax rates in Great Britain were greatly reduced by Margaret Thatcher in the 1980s. In 2003, Benjamin Netanyahu became finance minister in Israel and greatly cut taxes and the size of the public sector. In the 1990s, India greatly reduced taxes and removed many socialist restrictions on the economy and has been growing much faster. In all of these cases, the democratic process led to great falls in the size of the government sector, and in all cases the economy grew rapidly after the cut in the size of government and, as mentioned above, most of these countries are now high on the "freedom" index.

All of these countries had large government sectors but remained democratic, and all used the democratic process to reduce the size of the government. In all cases, the economy grew much faster after the government was reduced in size.

So it appears that there is a paradox. Countries can be socialist but non-democratic, such as the Soviet Union, China, Cuba, and Venezuela, or democratic but non-socialist, such as the Nordic countries, Britain, and Israel. This is because democratic countries, while they may create a large government sector by voting, ultimately use voting to shrink this sector. In the U.S., the share of government spending has increased from about 7 percent of GDP in 1902 to about 40 percent today, with no major backlash (yet).

If voting is not allowed or not meaningful, the next alternative is protest and demonstrations. It is relatively easy to vote out an undesired government in a fair election. It is much more difficult to organize demonstrations, and so things must get worse before we see demonstrations. Even then, demonstrations will often not work. The government controls the police and military, and so can put down any demonstration. Nonetheless, demonstrations serve to indicate to the government that the people are unhappy. As I write this in winter 2020, there are ongoing major pro-freedom demonstrations in Hong Kong and Iran. When you read this, you may know how the issue was resolved.

The final stage is outright rebellion. This is extremely difficult because socialist governments forbid citizens from owning arms, therefore, it is quite difficult to withstand armed police or military. Thus, a socialist regime that does not allow free voting can exist for a long time, even if the people are oppressed and unhappy.

FORMER SOVIET COUNTRIES

Soviet Russia was associated with two types of countries: the sixteen socialist "republics" which comprised the Soviet Union (The Union of Soviet Socialist Republics) and the Russia-controlled satellite countries. Since the collapse of the Soviet Union, these countries have gone separate ways. Some have become quite free: Estonia is 15th on the list, and Georgia is 16th. Others are spread throughout the list. Russia is 98th. Some countries have done economically better than others, with, as you might guess, the freest countries having the largest gains in income.

So you are freer in a capitalist regime. If a society chooses socialism and if it remains politically free, it is likely to return to capitalism. Mr. Sanders talks about "democratic socialism." This apparently means that a socialist country can revert to capitalism. However, there is a good chance that a socialist regime will not remain free, in which case it may be stuck in socialism for a long time, even if the citizens would like to move to a market economy.

CHAPTER 3

GOVERNMENT PROVISION OF GOODS AND SERVICES

You might say, "So what? I am paying higher taxes, but I am getting services from the government, so isn't it a wash? Doesn't it come out even?"

COSTS OF GOVERNMENT PROVISION OF GOODS AND SERVICES

This raises several important issues. First, whatever goods and services the government provides are more costly and less desirable than those provided by the market. This is because the government of necessity lacks incentives to use resources efficiently. Examples: In a managerial job at the Federal Trade Commission, I suggested to my boss that we should use more computers and fewer secretaries. He thought it a great idea. But then he told me that secretaries were under a different budget classification than were machines, and we could not substitute one for the other. We thus lost a chance for a real cost savings. No private firm would handcuff itself in that way. Additionally, it is virtually impossible to fire anyone in the government. In one government job, a high-level employee spent much of her time for a year in documenting the failures of an incompetent worker in order to generate the paper trail to fire the incompetent. I only worked for two agencies for a few years, but I still observed substantial low-level inefficiencies. Inefficiencies such those and vastly larger ones exist throughout the entire government.

It is sometimes argued that the government can do things more cheaply because there are no profits in government provision. Although you may think "profits" is a dirty word, in fact profits provide the incentive for firms to be efficient. The lack of profits in government provision means that government lacks the incentive to be efficient. (Colleges and universities as "non-profits" also have weak incentives for efficiency, as you have probably noticed in your career as a student.) In the private sector there are incentives to reduce costs of production. If costs are reduced, profits increase for two reasons. First, the firm will make more money per unit because each unit costs less to make. Second, part of the cost reduction will be passed on to consumers through lower prices, and so the firm will sell more units.

You might be surprised by my saying that part of the gain from reduced costs will be passed on to consumers as lower prices. Won't greedy capitalists keep all the savings? But it is in the interest of the firm itself to pass on part of the savings. The firm will pass on part of the cost reduction not because it is kind or nice, but because the mathematics of profit maximization requires reducing prices if costs fall, therefore passing on part of the savings to consumers. That is, simply, a firm will make even more profits if it passes on part of the cost savings to consumers. Here is an example: Go to Amazon and look up any book—say, this one. There are in general two or three ways to buy a book. Consider paperback and Kindle. It costs less to produce a Kindle book (actually, it costs virtually nothing, once the file is created) than to produce a paperback book. And lo and behold, the Kindle book is (almost) always cheaper than the paperback. This is not because Amazon or the publisher are trying to conserve paper or to be nice to consumers. Rather, it is because Amazon and the publisher make more money by pricing an electronic book at a lower price, because it costs less to produce. (If you want to better understand this point, I suggest a basic economics course.)

Another incentive for firms to reduce costs is competition. Any firm that can reduce costs can get a jump on the competition, thereby increasing sales. There is no competition in government. Consequently, this important incentive is lacking.

Also, if a firm invents something new, and the new product is successful, then it will make money because its sales will increase. Thus, firms have incentives to be innovative, both in terms of reducing costs and in terms of improving products. Because there are no profits in government and because there is no competition, governments do not have these incentives. For example, airplane technology is continually evolving, but the Air Traffic Control system, run by the government, is notoriously outdated and inefficient. There have been many unsuccessful efforts to improve the efficiency of this system, but none have worked.

The government itself is aware of this issue. In most cases, rather than produce something internally, the government allows private firms to produce and sell to the government. Although this process is not as efficient as it might be because government tends to use clumsy processes for hiring private firms, it is nonetheless more efficient than internal production.

For example, the military is aware of the inefficiency of government production and uses private firms to produce the products it uses, from uniforms to airplanes to aircraft carriers. The government procurement process is itself inefficient and costly because of excessive regulation of this system, but it is still better than actual government production would be. Of course, if we move towards socialism, the military might begin to produce its own stuff, with a corresponding negative impact on you, the future taxpayer.

Another example is highways. Again, in most cases the government has private contractors build highways rather than build them itself. There are inefficiencies in this process, but it is still better than the government itself building the roads.

One case where the government does provide a service itself is public schools. There is a lot of evidence that privately provided education is more efficient and produces better results than public schools, but teachers fight the privatization process, and it has been too slow.

In fact, in many cases, there are actually incentives for inefficiency in government production. As an example, consider the Postal Service. There are many ways that mail could be delivered more cheaply. But mail carriers are also voters and citizens, and there are some of them in every congressional district. Increasing efficiency would mean fewer postal workers, and postal workers and their families and friends would vote against any politician who proposed efficiencies, and their union would organize campaigns against reducing the number of workers. Similarly, there are more efficient ways of providing education to children than the monopolistic public-school system, but teachers and their unions are strongly opposed to programs such as vouchers that improve education but remove the monopoly power of teachers embodied in unions and exercised through the monopolized public school system. Other government employees also oppose programs that would reduce their incomes, and they oppose these programs as voters as well as employees. If we socialize additional activities—make them government programs—then we create additional voting blocks in favor of higher costs.

In the private sector, there are incentives to reduce the number of people needed to do some job, because this saves money. In the government, the incentives are often reversed. If some agency saves money, it goes back to the general government budget and does not do the agency any good. On the other hand, if the agency hires more people, taxpayers bear the costs, and the agency benefits by having more personnel. That means that managers are managing larger groups and are more likely to get promotions and pay increases. Indeed, the best theory of government agencies is that they attempt to become as large as possible. At the end of the year, if money is left over, the incentive is to spend it on something (anything) because if it is not spent, next year's budget will be reduced.

GOVERNMENT AND CHOICE

The second point is about government provision of goods and services. In a capitalist economy, you have lots of choices. For example, consider medical care, which many want to socialize as "Medicare for All" as discussed by Senator Sanders and other Democratic politicians. It is important to realize that Medicare for All will totally replace all existing medical plans. All employer-provided insurance will be eliminated, as will all private insurance. Most working Americans now receive their insurance from their employer, and most are happy with it, but Medicare for All will totally eliminate that insurance.

Under the current system, some doctors charge more and provide quicker and more personalized service. If this better service is worth the cost, you pay for it; if not, you don't. Some procedures are elective; do you want Lasik eye surgery to eliminate glasses or not? If you have cataract surgery (something that you don't care about now, but probably will in the future), do you want to pay more for a better lens, or are you content with the standard lens and glasses? Your knee is painful; do you fix it now or wait until it becomes more painful for a replacement? Are you willing to pay more for the brand-name drug, or are you happy with a cheaper generic? Do you want insurance that covers everything, or only catastrophic events, which is cheaper? In a market system (and even though it is imperfect, our current medical system has many market aspects left) you have these choices. Many employers (including the government) offer several health insurance plans to workers. Some are more expensive and offer better service; some are cheaper and offer less service. There is competition between plans and between providers, and you can choose. Medicare itself is a "one size fits all" system, but there are many providers offering supplemental insurance and many providers offering Medicare Advantage plans. During "open season," when consumers are allowed to change their plans, Medicare participants received daily advertisements for alternative plans.

A socialist system is "one size fits all," and you lose the ability to make these choices. Indeed, many of the socialist medical plans proposed by the left outlaw the private provision of medical insurance. The very rich would be able to travel to other countries to obtain services that would be forbidden in the U.S. There is already a world-wide market in "medical tourism," where people travel to other countries for services that are not available in their home country, and Medicare for All would greatly increase the size of this market. Indeed, I can envision clinics in Mexico staffed by U.S.-trained doctors providing a level of quality care that would not be available in the U.S. under Medicare for All.

Medicare for All will not create any new doctors or medical facilities. More people will be covered for more ailments than is currently the case. Some proposals require coverage for all immigrants, including illegal immigrants. There will be no co-pays, so people will seek medical attention for issues that they now ignore and that often cure themselves. Moreover, many doctors might choose to retire earlier than otherwise or work for clinics in other countries, because they will not want to be bureaucrats in a government-run system. If fewer docs are treating more patients for more conditions, then quality of care will necessarily be reduced. Moreover, Medicare for All would eliminate competition between insurance plans and between medical providers. We now rely on competition to control prices. Under Medicare for All there would be only one insurance provider, the government, and there would be no competition between providers, since all would effectively be government employees.

There is another point relevant for you as a young healthy person. In discussing medical procedures, I mentioned cataract surgery, knee replacements, and hospital stays. You don't care about any of these (unless they are important for your parents or grandparents) because you are young and don't use much medical care. These are important to old people (like me, which is why I know about them), and they are a significant part of the cost of the medical system. But in a socialized system, everybody pays for everybody else. That is, you would be paying for medical services for old people out of your income when you are young, when you don't need much medical care. (You already pay something in the form of Medicare payments withheld from your paychecks, but Medicare for All would greatly increase this cost.) This would be part of the increased taxes mentioned above. The Council of Economic Advisers (CEA) in the 2019 *Economic Report of the President* has estimated that Medicare for All would cost about $18,000 in additional taxes for every family in every year. This is money you would begin paying through taxes as soon as you got a job.

That is not all. Medical care is about 16 percent of current GDP. Under a Medicare for All system, this would all be paid for by taxes. Because taxes would be higher, there would be a reduced incentive to work. The CEA, using standard growth and income models, indicates that this reduction in work would lead to a 9 percent reduction in GDP. This is about $17,000 per household. Thus, socialized medicine would cost about $35,000 per family and would lead to reduced choice for patients. Actually, the cost would be higher because I have not considered the increase in cost of services due to the inefficiencies mentioned above.

A shortage is defined as a situation in which people want to buy more of some good or service *at the current price* but are unable to do so. In a market economy, we do not see "shortages." This is because market mechanisms adjust supply and demand to eliminate shortages.

Hypothetical medical example, market economy: People want to spend more time in the sun. Therefore, they want to buy more cancer-avoiding services from skin doctors (dermatologists). This increased desire for dermatologic services has several effects. First, the price of these services increases. Then more young docs decide to become dermatologists. Because these services are now more expensive, people take care to avoid using them, perhaps by staying out of the sun or using more protective lotions and hats. The market has adjusted. This goes on every day for millions of goods and services. The process is subtle and automatic, and all you see is that when you want to buy something, you can. The forces leading to equilibrium (no shortage) are one of the fingers of the "invisible hand" of the market.

But let the government run the medical market. Instead of market forces, government relies on central planning—the Commissioner of Medical Care decides how many dermatologists there will be. Since he is an old guy who wears a suit and hat and sits in an office all day, the Commissioner does not know that more people are going out in the sun, and he does not plan for enough dermatologists. He also sets the price for a dermatologist visit (in Sanders's version, the price is zero). As a result, there is no incentive for more young docs to become dermatologists. Lo and behold, there is now a shortage—you must wait two years to get an appointment. The socialist planning process does not have the self-correcting forces of the market, and so shortages can occur.

In a socialist system, there can be distortions in the other direction—surpluses, goods that do not sell at the current price. Continuing the example: Because people are spending more time in the sun, they are happier and so do not need the services of psychiatrists. In a market economy, fewer docs would become psychs. But because the Commissioner of Medical Care is a neurotic old guy, he does not see this and so orders an increase in psychiatrists. Because salaries are set by this same Commissioner, psychiatrists, while underemployed, do not observe any reduction in their incomes. Because there is no mechanism to adjust supply and demand, the surplus psychs can play more golf, and this leads to an increase in demand for dermatologists, which doesn't have any effect on supply.

Of course, this story is fanciful, but the point—that socialism lacks a mechanism for correcting shortages and surpluses—is quite real. In a market economy, the interaction of supply and demand would mean that prices would move towards what economists call "equilibrium"—that is, the amount demanded by consumers would move toward the amount offered by sellers. If buyers want to purchase more than is available, then they will bid up prices until the amount that buyers want to buy is equal to the amount that sellers want to sell. If sellers want to sell more than buyers want to buy at the current price, then price will move downward until the quantities are equal. Under socialism, prices are set by the government, and so this equilibrating mechanism is lacking.

Socialism would lead to government production of other goods and services in addition to health care. Senator Sanders mentions education, housing, retirement, jobs, and the environment. We could tell a similar inefficiency story about each, and I tell some of these stories later in the book. Socialism would lead to reduced quality and lower choice, increased costs, and market imbalance for any good that the government decides to produce. Paying for each of these goods would add substantially to your tax burden and reduce your real income.

For example, consider education, "the right to as much education as one needs to succeed in our society." This phrase is meaningless ("succeed" as a doctor? as a school-teacher? as a Walmart greeter?), but I am not going to address this issue. My guess is that if you are reading this book, you have finished a year or two of college and have paid for that year or two. Any law such as that mentioned by Senator Sanders will take probably take two or three years to fully pass and be funded; by then you have paid for your education and graduated. But you will now begin to pay for everyone else's education, and you will pay for others' education for the next forty-five years. Additionally, if government finances all education, there will be much less choice. Today there is a wide variety of colleges and universities, but government financing of education would reduce this choice. In the government-provided elementary and high school system, there is no choice—you go to the school in your district, unless your parents are willing to move or to pay for private school. Moreover, if people are not paying for their own education, there would be an incentive to study things that are fun, like music appreciation or the history of art, but that may not have much market demand. You might think that government would pay off your student debts. This is possible, but the increased taxes needed to finance everyone's college will follow you all your life, and you will pay off everyone else's debts.

For any good produced by government, there are two problems. First, the lack of market prices for the good itself and for its inputs means that producers would not be able to produce high-quality goods, even if they wanted to. Second, the lack of profits and the lack of competition means that producers would have no incentive to produce high-quality goods.

Although government provision has problems, there are some things that government must do because there are limitations on what the private sector can accomplish. The most important difficulty with the private market is what is called a "public good." A public good is a good that benefits everyone in the society, whether they pay for it or not. Someone who benefits but does not pay is called a "free rider." A classic example is national defense. The military protects everyone in the society. Currently, an important threat is terrorism. If there were no effort to prevent terrorism, everyone in the country would be a potential victim. Since everyone would benefit if anyone paid for anti-terrorism spending, each person would have the incentive to be a free rider and let others pay. The solution is to agree to force each of us to pay through the tax system.

Some other government activities are also due to free rider or public goods problems. We all breathe the same air, so clean air is a public good, as is clean water. If there is an epidemic, everyone can get sick, so public health is a public good. There are benefits to everyone from living in a society of educated people, so education is a public good and should be paid for by the government, although the government need not provide education.

For each of these, there are legitimate political debates as to the amount and form of government provision. There are also some additional activities paid for by government where there are arguments on both sides of the public good nature of the activity, such as subsidizing the incomes of the poor or construction of a national highway system.

Because government is inefficient and limited in its ability to determine exactly what people want, we should try to minimize the scope of those activities which the government undertakes. That is a major flaw of socialism: under socialism, government undertakes activities that are not public goods and that should be left to the market.

CHAPTER 4

SOCIALISM AND PANDEMICS

When I began writing this book, in 2019, the economy was doing extremely well. Unemployment was at a record low for virtually everyone—men, women, African-Americans, Hispanics, whites. Wages were growing. The stock market was at record levels. Much of the book was written with that in the background.

But as I was finishing the book, in 2020, the economy began to collapse. I do not know how the economy will be doing when you read this book. However, I do know that the economy will not be as healthy as it was before the pandemic. But unlike a "normal" recession, caused by economic factors, the 2020 collapse was due to a non-economic cause, a virus from China, not to any economic factors. While it might be possible to blame some recessions on market factors or policy errors, it is clearly impossible for the coronavirus recession. But even though the crash was not caused by economic factors, we can still ask what the effects of socialism or capitalism are on minimizing the harm from an unexpected event such as the coronavirus.

RESPONSE TO THE EPIDEMIC

We consider the Chinese response and the U.S. response, and what we can learn from these responses about the efficiency of a socialist system in a pandemic.

The Chinese Response

We do know that the virus began in China, a communist country. Moreover, it may be that the disease began in a government lab in Wuhan, and then spread perhaps to a "wet" market, a market where live animals are sold for food. (The thought is that it might have escaped from a lab studying bat viruses, not that it was engineered for biowarfare.) It is also possible that the virus started in the market itself, as claimed by the Chinese. (By the time you read this we may know the answer.) Socialist and communist governments tend to be top down governments, and generally do not put as much weight on individuals as do free economies and democratic societies. (For example, the only major nuclear accident was at Chernobyl, a Soviet run nuclear plant.) Labs in the U.S. and other market countries are more careful than the

Wuhan lab may have been. There is evidence that both Chinese and U.S. inspectors had found that the Wuhan lab violated numerous safety standards, so a leak from this lab is quite possible. So we do know that a socialist government is more likely to start a viral epidemic, and more likely to lie about it once it is started.

The first unrecognized case of coronavirus ("patient zero") was on November 17, 2019. In late December Chinese scientists sequenced the virus and learned that it was 87 percent similar to SARS, a previous harmful virus which spread from person to person. This led to a fear that this virus would also be harmful. However, the Chinese government initially lied about the possibility of an epidemic, and continually lied about its size. On December 27, officials ordered scientists to destroy all samples and remove all information about the new virus. On January 7, in a secret speech, Mr. Li indicated that a pandemic was likely. On January 16, officials indicated that the crisis was over and urged people to travel and participate in large public demonstrations, one of the many falsehoods from the Chinese government. Millions of people were to travel to celebrate the lunar New Year on January 25. On January 24, group travel was banned in China but not overseas. The Chinese government also banned many foreign reporters and threatened scientists and others who attempted to track the virus. In February, the Chinese Government banned a game, Plague, Inc., because it could draw attention to the possibility of a plague. Wuhan is a travel center, both for rail within China and for air internally and internationally. This contributed to the spread of the virus.

So: It would have been possible to stop the virus as early as December 26 or 27, when the virus was relatively small and localized. By late January, when it had already begun spreading around the world, it was too late. The Chinese government, a communist government which put relatively little weight on the welfare of its citizens, was willing to sacrifice many to try to keep information secret. This meant that both Chinese and non-Chinese doctors, scientists, and health officials at first underestimated the level of danger from the virus.

U.S. Government Response: The FDA and the CDC

What about the response once the virus reached the U.S.? Because the virus spreads exponentially, (one person contaminates two people, who each contaminate two more...) an extremely fast response (which would have slowed down the virus before it had time to spread) was crucial. There were possibilities for a better organized and quicker response, which would have led to fewer deaths. From the actual response, we know that if the U.S. had had a socialist government run health agency, as would be true if the country were socialist, the response would actually have been much worse than the actual response, and many additional Americans would have died. This is in part because the government agencies that participated in the response actually made the situation worse at every turn, and the only forces that improved the situation were the private market participants, such as the pharmaceutical firms and non-federal labs. Private labs and some state government labs (generally run by hospitals associated with large state universities) provided most of the early research, slowed down by Federal agencies. In a socialist system, there would have been no corrective to the errors of the government lab, and so the epidemic would have gotten much worse.

Accordingly to the epidemiologists, the most important input for initially containing an epidemic such as the coronavirus is testing. Testing enables health officials to quarantine those who are contagious, and to trace their contacts to find additional victims and quarantine them. Countries such as South Korea and Taiwan that have quickly deployed robust testing regimes have done the best job of containing the virus. The U.S. has done a very poor job of testing. Between early February and mid-March, the U.S. lost several important weeks because tests were not available. Because of the exponential growth of the virus, slowing down the virus when it is beginning is extremely important.

Although the story is more complex, fundamentally what happened is that the two Federal agencies that should have been controlling the virus each committed a major error, and the combination of these errors is what led to the epidemic. The Food and Drug Administration

(FDA) is responsible for approving diagnostic tests such as possible tests for coronavirus. The Center for Disease Control (CDC) is in charge of finding and controlling epidemics and contagious diseases. (The control of contagious diseases is one of the most legitimate functions of government.) However, the FDA allowed only the CDC to develop and validate a test for the virus, and the CDC screwed it up. Thus, for several crucial weeks, there was no valid test for coronavirus in the U.S.

The FDA is responsible for certifying all diagnostic tests (and new pharmaceuticals.) It can take a up to a decade or more for a test to be certified. The FDA believes that an inaccurate test is worse than no test, and so seeks a high level of certainty in approving a test. This may be correct in normal times, but clearly during a major health crisis costs and benefits have changed radically. (The FDA is also overly restrictive in approving new drugs.)

Some non-federal labs were working on potential tests for coronavirus in December 2019. On January 31, 2020, the Secretary of HHS (Health and Human Services, the parent of the FDA) declared the virus to be a "Public Health Emergency." This triggered another requirement: anyone proposing a test was required to obtain an "Emergency Use Authorization" (EUA) from the FDA. This required that tests developed by private or state labs obtain an additional certification from the FDA. Although the EUA is an "Emergency" authorization, issued in response to a public health "Emergency," it actually makes it more difficult to obtain an authorization by requiring additional testing of the test. Moreover, this testing and the associated bureaucratic requirements are not a formality; they can add much additional time to obtaining permission. Because of this additional testing required, many labs that had been working on a test or actually had a test available put their programs on hold, and many others that were planning to begin work on a test did not. In trying to get a EUA, one researcher who was working on a test at the University of Washington in Seattle was required to physically mail information to the FDA after sending it electronically. He was also told to show that his test could distinguish between another virus, SARS, and the coronavirus. However, he was unable to obtain a sample of the SARS virus since the CDC would not release it. So the FDA required that he validate his test against another virus but the CDC would not release the additional virus.

On February 3, the CDC was issued an EUA from the FDA. This allowed the CDC to send materials to other labs which would have allowed additional patients to be tested. However, the CDC test (the only test allowed in the U.S. at that time by the FDA) did not work. The best thought now is that the CDC test was contaminated by another virus.

Finally, on February 29, the FDA allowed some private labs meeting high standards to begin testing, but few had developed a test since they were not allowed to use them, so it took longer to get full testing up and running than it normally would have. Moreover, only about 5000 labs met the excessively high standards the FDA set, out of about 260,000 labs in the country. Finally, on March 16, the FDA allowed all labs to run tests. However, the entire process slowed down the development of tests and the testing by several crucial weeks, while the virus was spreading rapidly.

The error here is clear. In approving any diagnostic test, there is a tradeoff between speed and accuracy. If a test is approved more quickly, it is more likely that the test is less accurate. (A test for a disease may err by finding someone healthy who has the disease or finding them sick when they are healthy.) Testing the test more thoroughly will make it more accurate but will take longer and will mean that some people are not tested as soon as otherwise. Normally, the speed at which someone is tested by a new test is not particularly important since there are usually existing alternatives. However, during the rise of an epidemic, speed becomes all important because of the exponential rate of growth of the epidemic. The FDA was initially unable or unwilling to change the terms of the regulatory tradeoff even though the terms of the health tradeoff had shifted radically, in favor or a greatly increased value of speed. On March 16, when the FDA allowed more widespread use of tests, it issued a press release praising itself because "This action demonstrates the FDA's ability to pivot and adapt as the situation warrants in light of a public health emergency." In other words, the FDA claims that it deserves great praise for speeding up the testing process by getting out of the way.

The next step in recovering from the pandemic is to begin testing people for immunity by looking for antibodies in the blood which indicate immunity. I am writing this on April 21, 2020. It so happens that yesterday, April 20, the FDA, CDC and National Institute of Health (NIH) issued a joint statement. This statement indicates that the agencies are apparently going to be much less restrictive in allowing and approving these tests than was the case for the initial tests for the disease, so perhaps government agencies do have the ability to learn. We shall see.

Lessons

With respect to socialism and capitalism, there are three lessons here. The three critical issues in the epidemic were: safety and care in dangerous activities associated with the virus; freedom of information; and competition in developing remedies.

With respect to carefulness: China is a communist, not socialist country. Neither a capitalist nor a socialist country has generated an epidemic. So we know that democratic market countries are at least as careful as socialist countries. Communist countries are much less careful. Several potentially disastrous flu epidemics (Asian flu, Hong Kong flu, SARS) probably began in China, and Chernobyl (the explosion in a nuclear reactor that killed many people) occurred in communist Ukraine. We do not have any evidence of a socialist country beginning a disaster. So we know that communist countries are less careful with human lives than free market countries, but we have no real evidence about socialist countries. With respect to information, the situation is similar: we know that China concealed crucial information which made a small accident into a major international disaster. Not only has the U.S. not concealed information about the epidemic, but President Trump and the major health officials are on national TV every night discussing the epidemic and answering questions from the press. Indeed, there is an argument to be made that we are getting too much information.

It is the third area, competition in developing remedies, we have strong evidence that market economies dominate. This is because, as discussed above, at the beginning of the epidemic the U.S. acted like a socialist country. There was a government agency (the FDA) which exercised the power to decide who was allowed to make tests, and a government agency (the CDC) which had the monopoly right to produce tests. It so happens that in this case the CDC messed up, which made a bad situation into a disaster, but even if this had not occurred, granting one entity the sole right to produce the tests for coronavirus was a serious mistake by the FDA. First, if there is only one producer, then there is a significant chance for an error, such as actually occurred, and no backup. Second, if many entities are producing tests, then some may be better or quicker than others. Once the market was opened up, there have been frequent news stories about quicker and cheaper tests being made available. The latest news is a test that can be administered at home. These tests were not developed by the government.

AFTER THE PANDEMIC

The pandemic and the measures taken in response—the shutting down of the economy—have caused great harm to the economy. Many businesses have closed, and many have gone bankrupt. The value of capital assets and the amount of wealth in the economy have fallen. Unemployment has reached twenty-two million in April and may go much higher. It will be a major task to put the economy back together.

When this process begins, there is no doubt that the left will claim that the task is so complex that substantial government planning and intervention will be needed to accomplish the task, and that the job is too complicated for markets to work. I can predict this reaction from the left because the left does not understand the power of markets and *always* thinks any task is too complex and needs government assistance.

In fact, the opposite is true. The more complex a task is, the more important it is to leave it to the market and the more difficult it is for the government to handle it. This is because a complex task is one with lots of moving parts that must be coordinated. In a planned effort from the government, one decision maker will try to coordinate all of these parts but will not have the information needed. In a market response, each part will be controlled by someone with a deep knowledge of that part and incentives through prices to use it efficiently. Markets respond to prices, and prices convey a huge amount of information very efficiently. Governments attempt to benefit "social welfare" and respond to political forces. Both of these provide murky signals and generate little useful information, so the process does not work well at all.

Markets are driven by forces of supply and demand and so errors are self-correcting. Government actions ignore supply and demand, and errors are often self-magnifying. Errors occur in market economies but are much more likely to occur in socialist economies.

For evidence, consider some natural disaster, such as a flood or hurricane. Because of disrupted transportation channels, there will generally be a "shortage" of gasoline. In this circumstance, the efficient outcome would for the price of gasoline to increase. An increase would be the market response if the market were left alone. In the short run, this increase in price will efficiently ration the gasoline. That is, those who value the gasoline the most—are willing to pay the most for it—will get the gasoline. In the medium run, the increase in price will lead to an increased supply as sellers will make greater efforts to get their trucks to the area where prices are higher. In the longer run gasoline retailers will anticipate that in the event of a disaster, they will be able to raise prices, and so will carry larger inventories, particularly in hurricane prone areas. When the government (usually state) does not allow "gouging" and fixes the price, all of these beneficial effects are lost.

The coronavirus is essentially a large natural disaster. Many goods will be in short supply, and many suppliers will have gone bankrupt. To the extent that the government is involved, some of these goods will have prices regulated by government and so the beneficial effects of price increases, in ending the shortages more quickly, will be lost. The goods whose prices will be fixed are likely to be those goods which are politically salient. The government may also dictate terms on which bankrupt business may reopen or may get financing to enable reopening.

Government may also interfere by requiring higher quality for some goods and services. For example, many people in retirement or assisted living homes have died from the virus. The government may well decide that this is because these homes did not meet adequate standards and may impose high safety standards. But there is no point in making retirement communities safe enough to survive a 100-year event, and the increase in costs caused by such standards will price many elderly individuals out of perfectly adequate housing.

In fact, even before the virus, government often requires levels of safety that add costs and actually reduce safety. For example, there is evidence that higher standards for accident (tort) law increase costs of products like drugs and also medical services to the point where safety is actually decreased, and accidental deaths are increased. There is evidence that safety standards in automobiles convinced the drivers that cars were safer and led to more careless driving and may actually have increased accidents.

The reopening will be complicated because the goals will be to open the economy without "excessive" deaths, where no one really knows the meaning of excessive or the rate at which different terms for reopening, such as the best level for social distancing, will lead to deaths. There is evidence that almost all the fatalities from the virus are old people (like me). Thus, it might be possible to allow reopening but require or urge old people to remain isolated. Whether this is actually correct and whether it is politically acceptable is still unknown.

Because the increased safety regulations associated with the virus will add costs, there may be an argument for relaxing other regulations to reduce costs. For example, the FDA regulations on emergency testing actually delayed testing during an emergency, and should be removed. It may also be possible to relax restrictions on scope of practice for non-physician health practitioners, such as physician's assistants and nurse practitioners. It may also be possible to relax state restrictions on physicians licensed in one state practicing in another. All of these regulations and numerous others add costs to medical care and provide little if any health benefits. This is not the place for it, but another book could be written (and many have been) about excessive regulation. Many of these should not exist anyway, but the virus may create an excuse or justification for eliminating them.

So while the coronavirus was not caused by an economic event, there are indications that such an event is more likely in a communist country than in a market economy. Moreover, government agencies, even in a free economy, mishandled this event, and in a socialist economy where there were no backups to the government, the harm might have been much greater. The coronavirus may also create an opportunity to eliminate many costly but useless regulations.

CHAPTER 5

WHY ARE WE RICH?

CAPITALIST PROPERTY RIGHTS

Assuming that we get out of the coronavirus mess, you are in the luckiest generation that has ever lived. You are luckier than I am because you will live to see many technological innovations that I will not see. I cannot predict what all of them will be, just as I could not predict the internet or the cell phone. I do predict that you will have a much longer and healthier life than I will. I sometimes fear that I will die just before the innovation that lets us live to 150 is invented.

Unless we choose policies that will screw it up.

In all dimensions, you live better than kings of the past, even the ones who lived happily ever after. You live better even than rich people of fifty or a hundred years ago.

Consider where you live. Even if you live in an average house, you have hot and cold running water and modern plumbing, and probably more than one bathroom. You have heat in the winter and air conditioning in the summer, both at the touch of a switch (or, if you have a Nest, without even touching a switch). You have a 60-inch color TV with a sound bar. You can talk to anyone in the world instantly. You can physically visit them in a few hours. You can learn almost anything without moving, either from your phone, your computer, or your Kindle. You have interesting foods easily available, both in grocery stores and in restaurants, and the food can be delivered if you want. Your OK Google or Alexa can provide you with recipes. You have an automobile at your disposal, either your own or an Uber. You can order almost anything from Amazon without leaving your desk. You can hear millions of songs, watch thousands of TV shows and movies, and read books, including this one. You can also play complicated games on your TV or Xbox One. Like our ancestors, you may be worried about food, but unlike most of our ancestors, you are worried about eating too much food, not about starving because of a famine.

Why do we have so many options? Why are we so rich? The answer is in our economic and legal institutions. Without capitalism, we would still be living as poor subsistence farmers with a low life expectancy and a fairly miserable life.

The most important institution is property rights. A property right is the right to use and transfer some piece of property and to exclude others from using it. English law, which is the basis of American law, provided protection for property. (America improved on English property rights.) This protection is twofold. First, your neighbors cannot take or trespass on your property. ("Property" includes anything that can be owned, not just land.) If you cannot stop them, the police will come to your aid.

Just as important is protection from the government itself. In the U.S., the government is limited in its ability to take your property. The Fifth Amendment to the Constitution reads in part: no person shall be "deprived of ... property without due process of law; nor shall private property be taken for public use, without just compensation." This amendment is extremely important. First, it requires that any property the state wants to take must be for a "public use." Second, the rule requires that "just compensation"—the value of the property—be paid. Both of these issues can be and often are litigated. Is the use public? Is the compensation just? But it is important that the courts, where the issues are litigated, are separate from the executive branch, which wants to do the taking. Remember "checks and balances?" The point is that government cannot simply take your property; it must go through a contestable legal process and prove that it has a legitimate purpose. Historically, kings had the power to take whatever they wanted, often including people, and some dictators still have that power.

The legal system in the U.S. and the rest of the developed world is aimed at making the most efficient use of property. The protection of property rights means that you can use your property however you want, within some limits mostly related to public nuisance (for instance, burning leaves in your backyard). More importantly, you can improve your property—for example, build a building on it—with no fear of loss through unpaid government confiscation. This means that we undertake massive investments without worrying that the government may take the building.

In addition to property rights in land, there is an important class of property rights called "intellectual property." Intellectual property includes patents, copyrights, trademarks, and trade secrets. This class of rights protects inventions and has other benefits.

A patent is the right to an invention. This invention may be a physical machine or a chemical entity, such as a drug. Because the U.S. and other Western countries provide patent protection, people and business are willing to invest thousands or millions of dollars to create new products and new inventions. I don't need to tell you what these inventions are—you live with them every day of your life. Your parents or grandparents are alive and healthy because of pharmaceuticals. We would all be poorer without patents. Indeed, most of us wouldn't have been born since patents (on seeds, fertilizer, pesticides, farm equipment) enable us to produce more food and other goods necessary to support our large population.

A copyright protects original works of authorship including literary, dramatic, musical, and artistic works, including this book. Again, this creates incentives to create works. I would not be writing this book without a copyright to protect my royalties (this will no doubt be a best seller and make me rich), and the publisher would not publish it without similar protection. With the beginning of electronic copying, there were difficulties in establishing and protecting copyrights in music, but those issues have been worked out, and lots of new music is created. (Actually, there has been no good music since the Beatles, but some still mistakenly value the new music.)

Trademark protects names and logos for products. This provides incentives for manufacturers to produce quality products. For example, when you buy a Coke you know what you are getting. When you see a McDonald's sign, you know what the food will be. In some illegal markets, such as illegal drugs, there are no trademark protections, and sometimes harmful products are sold, at least according to *Law and Order*.

A trade secret is a method of production that is kept secret by the company and receives some protection as a trade secret. For example, if an employee quits and brings your trade secret to a competitor, you may sue.

Contract law allows the exchange of property rights. This is important because it enables property to move to its highest-valued uses. Tort (accident) law protects property from accidental and sometimes intentional damage.

An additional and very important form of wealth is "human capital"—the amount invested in skills and training. This is paid for in a variety of ways. Some is provided by schools. Some we acquire ourselves. An important cost of human capital is the opportunity cost of the time we spend getting educated, whether by going to school or studying at home. Some is provided by employers, often financed by reduced wages during the learning period. Much of our income is returns on investments in human capital, and so income taxes are a tax on this investment. We mostly have freedom to take whatever job we want, and to move if we want, so we are free to use our human capital.

It is because of the protections of property rights that free market economies such as the U.S. are so wealthy. I want to emphasize this point. You have lived your entire life in a rich capitalist system—plenty of food, automobiles, decent housing, TVs, stylish clothing. It may be difficult to imagine a world without these things, but they do not come from the Tooth Fairy. They exist because we live in a capitalist system with protected property rights.

SOCIALIST PROPERTY RIGHTS

Socialist economies provide little if any protection of property rights. Socialism is defined as government ownership of the means of production. If private parties now own the means of production, and if the government is to own them, then the government must take them from those who own them. For example, socialism in Venezuela began with the government seizing the oil wells.

The main current socialist proposal, Medicare for All, will essentially take the human capital rights from physicians and other health care providers. By nationalizing the medical system, physicians will be forced to work for government wages. Hospitals will also be socialized. If physicians' compensation and freedom are lost, then fewer people, or less competent people, will become doctors. A socialist health care system will almost certainly fix prices for pharmaceuticals and medical equipment, and so reduce the incentive for creation of new remedies. This may mean that the invention leading to 150-year lives will not be created after all in a socialist system.

Other parts of the socialist program as proposed by Sanders and others will require much higher taxes, and this level of taxation will have many of the effects of socialism, even if some remnants of private property are left. As discussed elsewhere in this book, high taxes will discourage investment and innovation, and will change our system in many undesirable ways. If government can take property at will, then property owners will have greatly reduced incentives to improve property. High taxes are essentially a form of taking human capital and will have the harmful effects of any other lack of protection for property rights.

Socialist and environmental property rights are discussed in more detail later in this book.

CHAPTER 6

SOCIALISM AND WORK

Besides determining your income, your job is itself an important component of your life. Do you enjoy your work, or is it boring and tedious? Do you look forward to going to work each morning, or do you dread it? Do you feel like you have accomplished something worthwhile, or that you have just put in time? Do you like your co-workers and enjoy their company, or are they a bunch of turkeys (see *Dilbert*)? Is your boss nice and understanding, or a Scrooge who only wants to get the maximum money out of you and who doesn't care about your feelings or needs? If you are unhappy, can you easily leave your job? Remember, you will be working about two thousand hours a year for forty-five years, so all of these characteristics are very important.

You have observed your parents and the parents of your friends and perhaps relatives or others in the labor force. You have dealt with people doing their jobs—teachers, doctors, salespeople, mechanics, servers—and have observed them working. You have watched TV shows which give some idea of work, although it is somewhat distorted. (You are more likely to be killed on the job on TV than in the real world.) You may even have had a part-time or summer job, so you have some direct personal experience with work. As a result, you probably think you have a pretty good general idea of what work is like and perhaps what sort of job you would like to have.

Forget everything you think you know about jobs. Everything you have observed is in a capitalist free market system. As we move towards a socialist system, the very nature of work and of jobs will change. The further we move towards socialism, the more work will change, but the changes being proposed now by proponents are enough to lead to major modifications in work. Some changes being proposed are some version of national medical care, such as Medicare for All; complete public support for higher education; and increased taxes to achieve a more equal income distribution. As the economy becomes more socialist, more and more people will work for the government. It is estimated that if we adopted all of Bernie's proposals, then 50 percent of the workforce would work for the government.

I have purposely not used the word "free" to characterize health care and education provided by the government because it is important to realize that these goods and services are *not* free. They must be paid for by someone, and that someone is the taxpayer. Once you enter the labor force and begin working, *you* will be that taxpayer.

If we adopt Medicare for All or any of its cousins, then everyone working in the health sector will effectively be a government employee. At first, the government may allow some freedom, but there will be tremendous pressure to control costs, and this will soon lead to decisions to control health workers and reduce their salaries. For example, health workers can now freely change jobs for higher pay or better working conditions. Under Medicare for All, government will establish a scale for health workers (much like the GS scale for government employees that exists today), and, even if movement from job to job is allowed, the benefits of moving will be greatly limited because jobs will be on the same pay scale. This is another source of inefficiency.

In general, working for the government is different from working for a private firm. The simplest way to describe the difference is that government is much more bureaucratic. While every workplace has rules, government has many more rules, and penalties for breaking them may be higher than in the private sector. It is more difficult to get anything done in the government. I was a fairly senior manager in two agencies, but I still had to get clearance from two or three people before I could do anything, and even then there were many more levels before anything would be actually accomplished. My staff had to get clearance from an additional two people, including me, and these were all PhD economists. In my university jobs, I had complete freedom to write and publish what I wanted and to teach what I wanted. I do some consulting, and I am free to send whatever I want to the client, who must approve it. (As the song says, "You Gotta Serve Somebody.")

Another important difference is that there is little room for initiative in government work. This is because government work is highly "risk averse." Consider an employee who has a new idea in a private firm. If the idea works, the firm will make money and will reward the employee, sometimes with a large bonus, a major promotion, or both. It is sometimes even possible for the employee to leave and start his/her own business. There is also a downside—if the idea does not work, the employee may be penalized or even fired. But if the employee is confident enough, he/she might still try the idea.

Now consider the same situation in government. If the idea works, so what? There is little or no return from an innovation in government because there is no money to be made. Conversely, if the idea fails, the person who suggested it and his/her boss may be penalized. For example, Congress may hold hearings to examine the inefficiency of trying new things that don't work. Politicians running against the incumbent may use this as an example of bad management.

In 2003, the Defense Advanced Research Projects Agency (DARPA), an important pioneer in the internet and many other advanced technologies, proposed a prediction market based on the trading of futures contracts in political developments in Middle East countries. Many private firms have set up such markets in outcomes relevant to the firm, and they have been valuable and useful. These markets allow those with special knowledge to utilize this knowledge, with real money on the line. There are also such markets in political outcomes, such as presidential elections. However, Congress vetoed this DARPA proposal, and a very smart public official, John Poindexter, was forced to resign. I imagine subsequent heads of DARPA have been more careful (more risk averse) in their proposals.

Because there is little payoff for initiative or risk taking, government tends to attract workers who are themselves risk averse. Government jobs are secure, and there are well-established benefits, so workers who value these aspects but put little weight on major promotions tend to work for the government. These workers are not selected for their ability to come up with major innovations.

Another possibility today is that someone will work for the government for a while and then leave for better opportunities. I myself followed this pattern: I worked for a few agencies, then left for a consulting business, then for a university job (which was my original pre-government employment). Virtually every government job has a corresponding non-government job that ambitious government workers can get. Some leave for these jobs; others, the more risk averse, stay in government. As government takes over a larger share of the economy under socialism, the incentive to leave and the possibility of leaving will be reduced. This means that individuals who plan on working for the government for a while and then leaving will not do so, and so more risk-averse people will work for the government. For example, the increase in taxes discussed above will reduce the incentive to take risks and leave government. Because it will have a monopsony (monopoly on the buyer's side), government may make it more difficult to get another job in a related industry. Government will be staffed by more and more risk-averse individuals.

The relation between socialism and risk taking is very important for many aspects of our lives, not just labor markets, and I will discuss it later.

Working for the government is rule governed. But so is dealing with the government. We have all had the experience of an employee of a private firm bending the rules in order to make our life easier. But government employees are much more rigid. There is no incentive to bend the rules because government employees do not care if they get more business and cannot accept tips. The penalties for breaking the rules are much more severe in government. Think of what it would be like if health care were provided by employees of the Department of Motor Vehicles (DMV) or the IRS.

The point of this chapter for your lives is simple. If production of goods and services is shifted from private firms to government, costs will be higher and quality lower. You as a citizen will be made poorer because your taxes will increase to pay for government production, and you will be getting less for your tax dollars because government will not do as well as private firms.

FAILURE

There is another source of increased efficiency in the private sector relative to government. Oddly enough, this is the possibility of failure. Private firms can fail, and many do. According the Small Business Administration, about 30 percent of new businesses fail during the first two years, 50 percent fail in the first five years, and 66 percent during the first ten. Moreover, it is not only small new firms that fail. Of the Fortune 500 (the largest five hundred firms in the U.S. as chosen by *Fortune Magazine*), only sixty firms that were on the list in 1955 were still on the list in 2017. The other 440 firms either failed to grow, went broke, or merged.

Why is it good that these firms can fail? This has to do with the process that the great economist Joseph Schumpeter called "creative destruction." A private firm fails when it cannot generate enough revenue from consumers and perhaps investors to pay its bills. This means that consumers do not value the products produced by the firm enough to purchase enough products to generate enough revenue—or more simply, consumers do not want the stuff.

There are several reasons why a firm may go bankrupt. It may be that consumers no longer want the product that the firm makes. It may be that some other firm has figured out a way to produce the product at a lower cost or higher quality. It may be that the value of some resource that the firm uses—say, land—has become too valuable for the firm to continue in that location, and it may move or it may shut down as some more favorably situated rival takes over.

What happens when a firm goes broke? The resources tied up in the firm are freed for use by another firm. Workers are fired, and so become available to work in other firms whose products are valued enough to generate revenue to pay the firm's bills. The land and buildings that the firm occupied and the equipment that it used become available for other firms. Stockholders may get back some of their capital, which is then available for investment in other firms (although the fact that the firm failed may mean that there is not much capital left for stockholders). In other words, the failure of firms is a necessary step in the movement of resources to their highest-valued uses, and necessary for increasing productivity and increasing wages.

This process is all around us, and because of the increasing rate of technological change, it is accelerating. Because of online shopping, many retail stores are closing, creating vacancies. It is not clear what will happen to that formerly valuable space, but ultimately the resources will be used for some purpose. As Amazon was growing, many retail salespeople were laid off, but because unemployment was so low many of them obtained other jobs, perhaps as stock pullers at Amazon.

Private firms are often inefficient, and in many instances may be just as inefficient as government agencies. However, there are two differences. First, government agencies need not convince consumers to purchase their products. Government is funded by tax revenues, which ultimately depend on force. Second, there is no competition, so even if another firm would be more efficient, it cannot enter the market and compete with the government firm.

The Postal Service illustrates both points. In 2019, the Postal Service was due to lose $3.4 billion. This loss will be made up by taxpayers, who will pay it even if they do not use the Postal Service. They lose this money even though they have two forms of monopoly protection from the U.S. government. First, with a few exceptions, the Postal Service has a monopoly on first class mail. (They do compete for parcel delivery.) Second, even though you buy your own mailbox, no one except the Postal Service is allowed to use it. Much of the power of the Postal Service is political: every congressional district has postal workers who are also voters. No one else cares very much about the Postal Service (excerpt its competitors), and so standard political processes lead to the Postal Service remaining in business with its monopolies.

This sort of result is standard. When the government operates some business, the workers—who are also voters—resist any policies that will cost them their jobs. For another example, this is why teachers and teachers' unions are able to resist charter schools and vouchers for private schools, both of which would lead to much better education.

This means that if more businesses become government operated, there will be no market pressure for increased efficiency, and inefficient businesses will be able to continue operating. This will be a major source of inefficiency in a socialist economy.

CHAPTER 7

INEQUALITY AND THE DISTRIBUTION OF INCOME

Socialists are much concerned with income inequality and particularly with the rich—the 1 percent, the "millionaires and billionaires." While socialists advocate higher taxes to pay for their policies, many also seem to want higher taxes to reduce the incomes and wealth of the rich and to achieve more equality, independent of the need for taxes to fund policies. Income redistribution is the name for taxation used to take money from some people and give it to others. While there may be good reasons for this policy, we must understand that at bottom this is what is going on: we are taking from some to give to others. At current levels, this is not a major issue (we are willing to accept current levels of transfers), but if we greatly increase the amount of redistribution (Sanders: **"We must take the next step forward and guarantee every man, woman and child in our country basic economic rights ... the right to a decent job ...the right to a secure retirement"**), it could become one.

Income redistribution involves a fundamental trade-off between fairness and incentives. We must always keep this trade-off in mind in thinking about redistribution. On the one hand, we may feel sorry for the poor and feel that it is morally required or fair that we improve their incomes by transferring money or goods and services (housing, medical care, food) to them. On the other hand, any effort to do so involves a reduction in incentives. The reduction in incentives is at both ends of the income distribution. Any effort to improve the lot of the poor through transfers creates an incentive for them to work less. Moreover, any effort to tax the less poor to transfer money to the poor creates an incentive for the less poor to reduce efforts to increase their income, either by working less or by investing less. There are also significant administrative costs to redistribution. Those IRS guys are not working for free, nor are the welfare distributors and social security workers. There is no way to avoid these trade-offs and costs. When it comes to income redistribution, like most other things, "There is no such thing as a free lunch." This does not mean that we should ignore the plight of the poor, only that we must keep in mind the costs.

INCOME DISTRIBUTION AND INEQUALITY

Contemporary socialists believe that the distribution of incomes in capitalist societies is biased, and too much goes to the rich. The "distribution of income" is an abstraction. No one can observe the distribution. We can only observe our own income, guess about other people's incomes based on how they live, and read about the incomes of movie stars, sports figures, and CEOs. Moreover, the term "income distribution" is itself misleading. There is no pot of income to be distributed to citizens. Incomes are earned, not distributed, and more productive people earn higher incomes. A belief that income is distributed rather than earned is an example of zero-sum thinking. So rather than discussing income distribution, I am going to begin by discussing something you do observe—grade distribution. In some ways grades are like income.

Some people get good grades, some not so good. Students who get good grades work hard, are smart, or, ideally, both. We can decide how hard to work, but how smart we are is given, and there is not much we can do about it. But we always observe a distribution of grades in a class or school. A grade is not just a measure of your standing in a class or your performance on an exam; it is a measure of how much you have learned. An A student in a class has really learned more than a B student in the same class. The A student has been more productive in learning. Similarly, a smarter, harder-working person will earn more, because he/she is more productive for the employer.

Grades are like income in that we can "spend" grades. We spend high school grades to get into better colleges. We spend college grades to get into better grad schools or to get better jobs. Finally, at the end of the process, we spend grad school grades to get better jobs.

Now consider jobs and salaries. Just as better grades mean that we have learned more, so higher salaries mean that we are more productive. In a market economy, employers and markets pay us based on our productivity. Higher-earning individuals are more productive than lower-paid individuals. The point is that higher-income individuals ("millionaires and billionaires") are in fact rich because they have added a lot to society through their productivity. Although you don't see it, you are actually better off because these individuals make a lot of money and, as I show later, you would be worse off if they did not. This is because the ways in which the rich have earned their money have benefitted you.

IS EQUALITY GOOD?

Those who complain about the 1 percent or about millionaires and billionaires seem to believe that equality is itself good, and inequality is bad.

Think again of grades. Would it be good if a professor announced on the first day of class that everyone would get the same grade because he believes in equality? Everyone would get a B+. Clearly that would be a bad policy because few would study or even attend class. So grade equality would not be good because it would destroy incentives to learn. Income inequality is similar: we need some incentive to work hard and invest, and the chance of higher incomes is what drives productivity.

Here is another way to view the same issue: Assume there are two islands. On island Equal, everyone has the same income, $30,000 per year. On island Unequal, 99 percent of the population has an income of $40,000, and the other 1 percent has an income of $1,000,000 per year. Everything else is the same on both islands—the same goods are available in the same stores at the same prices. Clearly island Unequal is more unequal than island Equal, but by any reasonable standard, life is better on island Unequal; everyone is better off on island Unequal. If you are shipwrecked and floating on a raft between Equal and Unequal, where would you chose to land?

There are two separate issues in discussing income distribution. One is equality. But more important is the income or welfare of the poor. Most of us are really concerned about the poor; we would like policies to make them less poor or enable them to enter the middle class and earn a reasonable income. Policies to reduce poverty are not the same as policies to reduce inequality, although some policies, such as higher taxes on the wealthy with the proceeds distributed to the poor, might do both. If we think they are always the same, then this is because we have a zero-sum view of the world: we view total income as fixed and think of it being "distributed" to different people; if Bill Gates gets more, someone else gets less. But this is not the correct view of the world. I discuss zero-sum thinking later.

PRODUCTIVITY AND WEALTH

In fact, the reason that some people are wealthier is because they (or perhaps their ancestors, if they have inherited wealth) were or are more productive than others. What does it mean to be productive in a market economy? To be productive means to provide some good or service that people value enough to pay for. That is, to be productive means that you are providing something that others value. Providing something that others value is the *only* legal way to earn income in a market economy. To see if great wealth is associated with high productivity, consider the ten richest people in the U.S., as chosen by Forbes Magazine:

- Jeff Bezos, Amazon

- Bill Gates, Microsoft

- Warren Buffett, Berkshire Hathaway

- Mark Zuckerberg, Facebook

- Larry Ellison, Oracle

- Larry Page, Google

- Charles Koch, Koch Industries

- David Koch, Koch Industries (Since deceased)

- Sergey Brin, Google

- Michael Bloomberg, Bloomberg LP

- (Keep this list in mind or bookmark it; we will return to it.)

Let us consider the productivity of each of these people. All of them are productive, and all have benefited you. You are of course familiar with Amazon, Google, Facebook, and Microsoft. You use their products every day. These companies are so new that the founders are still living unlike, say, Standard Oil (Rockefeller), Ford Motor Company (Henry Ford), Walmart (Sam Walton), or Apple (Steve Jobs), where the founders are dead. I don't need to convince you that these companies are highly productive. You and I could not live the lives we are living without them. Although the founders of these companies have made a lot of money, the amount they have made is only a small fraction of the total wealth and benefits they have created for consumers; they have moved us from island Equal to island Unequal, where they are really rich, but we are also much better off. The gains to consumers from the actions of these people is what economists call "consumer surplus"—the difference between what you pay for some product and what you would be willing to pay. For some of the goods mentioned, consumer surplus is huge, especially since the goods (Google, Facebook) are generally free.

A simple example of consumer surplus: I might be willing to pay five dollars for my first cup of coffee in the morning so I can function, but because of Keurig I can throw a fifty-cent pod in the machine and get a nice cup, with a consumer surplus of $4.50. A second example: I have just purchased a new computer; it cost $1,000. If I did not have any computer and there were only one available, I would probably pay a huge amount—at least $10,000 for it. I would probably pay much more since a computer will enable me to write this soon-to-be bestselling book. So my consumer surplus from this computer is at least $9,000—due to Steve Jobs, Bill Gates, and others (many of whom are rich) and to competition.

Consumer surplus may seem to be a technical curiosity of interest only to economists, but in fact it is the basis for the benefits of a market economy. That is, the fact that consumers routinely get more than they pay for is the reason that there are benefits created by a market economy. (For the technically minded, consumer surplus is the area below the demand curve above price. If you are interested in more details, consider an economics course.)

Warren Buffett is the most successful investor in the world. What does it mean to be a successful investor? It means that Mr. Buffett can successfully forecast which firms and industries are going to be successful (that is, productive) and then invest in them so that they can in fact succeed. He can make money by this investing, but he also contributes to the success—productivity—of the firms in which he invests. If he is wrong, he loses money. Since he has made a lot of money, he has not generally been wrong. He has been able to forecast what consumers will desire and has been able to help them fulfill these desires by investing.

Larry Ellison is the creator of Oracle, a highly (obviously, since he is on the list) successful software company involved in database creation and management, something that other firms use to make products better and cheaper, which benefits you indirectly. The Koch Brothers own and run Koch Industries, the only traditional firm on the list. It is involved in natural resources and chemicals, and numerous other production and manufacturing industries. The Koch Brothers have been phenomenally successful, which means they have reduced costs and improved products that we use in our everyday life or products that produce products that we use.

You may know Michael Bloomberg as a former mayor of New York, a candidate for president, and contributor to various causes. His wealth comes from creating Bloomberg LP, a major financial and other information company, which produces what finance professionals know and love as the "Bloomberg Terminal." This has increased the ability of financial professionals to make successful investments, and so to allocate capital in directions that have improved the economy and our lives.

These people and the others on the Forbes list are like the A students—smarter and more hard working than most of the rest of us. Some luck is probably involved, but all of these people had foresight, all faced major competition to achieve their success, and all provide goods or services that provide great benefits to consumers and to the economy. Though all of them are extremely rich because of their marketplace productivity, all have provided benefits to society much greater than the wealth they have accumulated. Moreover, what is true of the first ten is true of most or all the rest of the people on the Forbes list, although some people have become wealthy by inheriting money from those who were themselves productive. (The next three people on the list are heirs of Sam Walton, the creator of Walmart, which has been a major factor in improving the lives of consumers by reducing costs of goods and making more goods available.)

Recently, chief executive officers (CEOs) of large companies have seen large salary increases, which the socialists resent. We can explain this by the increasing value of CEOs and thus the increased competition for skills. Companies are becoming larger and more inter-national in scope. For example, Ford Motor Company is worth about $40 billion. If a CEO can increase its earnings by an additional 1 percent, then he is adding $400 million to stockholders. James Hackett, Ford Motor

Company's current CEO, earns about $17 million per year. So if he is competent (which is highly likely, given the competition for the job), then he is a bargain for the stockholders. Because a more efficient CEO will improve the general performance of the company, the products that you buy will generally be higher quality or lower in price if the company is better run.

SOCIALIST INCOME DISTRIBUTION

It might appear that incomes are more equal in socialist economies, but this is an illusion. The leaders in socialist regimes do very well, either in incomes or in power. For example, in the Soviet Union, there were special stores where high-quality imported merchandise was available to important political officials, called the nomenklatura. These officials also had access to better cars, health care, jobs for children, and housing. (Old joke: Brezhnev, a leader of the communist Soviet Union, is showing his mother his expensive, luxurious dacha (vacation home) with Western fixtures and many other expensive touches. His mother is impressed but asks, "But what if the Communists come back?")

In general, the powerful in socialist regimes do very well, while the rest do not. Moreover, the wealth of the elite in socialist regimes comes from their ability to tax and exploit the people. In a capitalist society, the wealth of the rich comes from their providing goods and services to the rest of us. Even though the ultra-rich (the 1 percent, the millionaires and billionaires) do well, the rest of us do OK, largely because of the stuff they make for us.

WHITE PRIVILEGE

Currently, one target of socialists is "white privilege." This "... is the societal privilege that benefits people whom society identifies as white." (Wikipedia.) Because many believe that whites (and more particularly, white heterosexual males) have benefitted from privilege, they feel that fairness demands that society should give an advantage to others—non-whites, women, gay people. Cries to "check your privilege" are commonly heard from "social justice warriors." Of course, this command assumes that the strength of an argument depends on who makes it rather than its validity and is a perfect example of the logical fallacy of an *ad hominem* argument.

The argument regarding white privilege is basically a zero-sum argument. It assumes that total output is fixed, and that it does not matter who gets particular jobs. Jobs are viewed as methods of distributing output, not as methods of production.

Those who believe in white privilege believe that it gives higher incomes and greater prestige to white people (or white men, or white heterosexual men). Thus, any benefits from being white must go through the labor market. But we know that ultimately the labor market pays for productivity—the amount of money that a worker adds to the bottom line of the hiring firm, or, to use economists' jargon, the worker's marginal revenue product.

So, to the firm, a worker is a source of profits, and firms will hire and pay based on maximizing profits. If firms pay white workers more, this must be because they are adding more to profits—they are more productive. A firm does not care where this productivity comes from; to the firm it is the bottom line as affected by the workers as they show up at the firm.

But even this does not take us all the way. To a worker, a job is a source of income and perhaps prestige. To an employer, an employee is a source of revenue and profits. But from the perspective of the economy, a job is a way of producing output. Firms can pay employees exactly because employees produce valuable output. This output is the basis of the firm's revenue and profits and the employees' earnings.

Thus, firms hire the most productive employees to maximize profits. A disproportionate share of these employees may be white males. But is that "fair"? Consider that employees produce output which is ultimately purchased by consumers of all genders and races. Remember that "consumer surplus" means that consumers get more than they pay for. All consumers—rich or poor, black or white, male or female—get consumer surplus from their purchases. Of course, rich consumers get more than poor consumers because they buy more. But the reason rich consumers are rich is because they are more productive.

If we replace more productive workers with less productive workers because we believe that more productive workers are "privileged" and that it is fair to replace them, then total output for the economy will be reduced, and all consumers—rich and poor—will buy less and get less consumer surplus. A few lucky workers may benefit from better jobs, but overall, lower income workers will lose because prices will go up, and they will be able to buy less.

So, in the end, the notion of privilege is just another way for the left to interfere with the functioning of the market economy, and like most such interventions, it will reduce output and will ultimately harm all consumers, privileged and non-privileged.

If we want to help lower-income people, the way is to increase their productivity. One way to do this is through education. Another way, more important in the short run, is to establish a set of rules and regulations that enable more people to find good-paying jobs. Redefining productivity as privilege will not change productivity and will have the effect of making everyone worse off.

So if we reduce inequality or if we allocate jobs based on characteristics other than productivity, we will reduce productivity and make everyone, including the benefited class, worse off.

CHAPTER 8

SOCIALISM, RISK-TAKING, AND INNOVATION

Most of us live fairly secure lives. We go to school, graduate, probably get married, take a job, and work for our forty or forty-five years. During that time, we may get some promotions and may change jobs a few times, but the pattern of our lives is mostly stable. Most of us are said to be "risk averse"—that is, we are willing to pay something directly or in foregone income to avoid risk. This is most clear when we pay money for insurance to avoid the consequences of unfavorable outcomes, but it applies to many aspects of our lives. For another example, we might be able to make a higher expected return by investing in risky stocks, but for most of us the chance of losing everything outweighs the chance of a higher return.

The same thing applies to jobs. Most jobs are fairly stable and pay relatively certain salaries. Some careers are riskier. We all know the example of Bill Gates, who dropped out of Harvard (and a certain high-paying career) to found Microsoft. That was clearly a risky decision, although it obviously paid off for Mr. Gates. But most of us prefer a steady paycheck and must be paid a premium to give up security. For example, at one point in my career I gave up the security of a government job to go to work for a consulting firm at a higher salary but a less secure job. Some engineers take secure jobs; others go to work for startups with lower pay but the possibility of great returns if the startup is successful. Some even begin startups. This is a risky choice, and many are unwilling to make it. We see the millionaires that come from the successful startups, but not the failures from the unsuccessful; however, there are many.

RISK TAKING AND THE RICHEST TEN

To see the importance of risk taking, let us consider each of the people on our list of ten. We will see that most of them took some risk in establishing or developing the company that became the source of their wealth.

Mr. Gates left Harvard to found Microsoft, a clearly risky decision. Jeff Bezos had a successful career on Wall Street before quitting to found a small online bookstore, which of course was again a risky bet. Warren Buffett was trained as an investor and had a career as an investor. While he may have made some risky investments, he had a fairly steady and successful career as an investor. Mark Zuckerberg founded Facebook while at Harvard, and it quickly became successful, so he did not seem to take much in the way of risks. Larry Ellison founded Oracle with a small investment and had difficult times at the beginning while competing with IBM. The Koch Brothers inherited an oil refining firm from their father, Fred Koch. They have built it into the second-largest privately-held firm in the U.S. by undertaking numerous investments, many of which were risky.

Sergey Brin and Larry Page created the Google search engine while in the PhD program at Stanford; they both left this program to further work on what became Google. (Before Google, the internet was not very useful because it was difficult to find relevant web pages.) At first, Google did not make any money (searches were free then as now, and there was no advertising revenue), but clearly the gamble ultimately paid off. Bloomberg had a successful career at Salomon Brothers, an investment bank, and upon leaving invested some of his wealth in creating what became Bloomberg LP, an information firm.

A STORY

Before proceeding, I want to tell a little story about a young socialist whom you may know. Call him Johnny.

He has found about socialism from readings on websites that he found using Google on his MacBook or PC. He likes socialism because he thinks he will get a lot of free stuff, maybe even including his tuition loans paid off. He has a Facebook or Instagram page where he discusses socialism with his buddies. He reads Tweets from various socialist heroes (Bernie Sanders, AOC). He posts pictures of socialist meetings on Instagram. He is getting ready to attend one now.

Before he goes to the meeting, he dresses in clothing purchased from Amazon and gets a meal delivered by Bite Squad, DoorDash, or Grubhub. He prints a backup copy of the directions on his HP printer. He calls or texts his buddies on his iPhone or Android phone to be sure to meet up with them at the rally. He orders an Uber or Lyft on his Echo and takes it to the meeting. On the way, he listens to music on Spotify, iTunes, or Pandora, or he may play Fortnite. (All of these use software developed by Microsoft or Oracle and chips from Intel, all owned by billionaires.) When he gets to the meeting, he and his buddies listen to speeches decrying the evils of capitalism and the sins of millionaires or billionaires, and he may give such a speech himself. On the way home, he prides himself on his dedication, and he is excited that so many are woke and have attended the rally against the evils of capitalism and inequality. Then, to relax, he watches a show on his 65-inch Sony TV through Roku with sound from a Bose sound bar.

Of course, I have cooked the books but not much. Each of the products I have mentioned—Mac, Facebook, Twitter, Instagram, Amazon, Bite Squad, DoorDash, Grubhub, iPhone, Android, Uber, Lyft, Spotify, iTunes, Fortnite, HP, Pandora, Microsoft, Oracle, Intel, Sony, Roku, Bose—are recent products of capitalism. Each are commonly used by you and your contemporaries, including those who are socialists. Each of these products are being continually improved. Each of these products relies on other products made by still other capitalists. Moreover, many of the founders of these businesses are billionaires. In Silicon Valley there are about seventy-five billionaires and thousands of millionaires. These millionaires and billionaires got to be millionaires and billionaires exactly by developing and improving the products that Johnny has used in getting to his speech about the benefits of socialism and the inequalities of capitalism.

Ask him which of the services discussed above he would be willing to give up, or think about this for yourself. Even simpler, think about which you would be willing to use in its current state, with no future improvement. There are few if any incentives for invention or improvement under socialism. While it may be possible to create incentives under socialism to continue to produce the same set of existing products more cheaply (although it is difficult to create the right set of incentives under socialism), there are few if any incentives to produce new innovative products or to improve products.

All the products mentioned above were produced by new firms; none were produced by existing firms. The incentive for establishing these firms and producing these products was in all cases the profits to be made by creating a successful company—the chance to become a millionaire or billionaire. Remove that incentive, and the intelligent and creative people behind the new companies will find something financially safer to do, and the products that Johnny relies on will never be produced. Even if we were to socialize the companies producing those products now so that they would continue to produce, there would be no incentive to improve the products.

All these products were invented and produced by smart engineers and businesspeople ("two guys in a garage") who had many safe options. All gave up these secure jobs to take a chance and start a new company. Of course, we know these companies because they were successful. There were also many startups that were unsuccessful. A Google search for "unsuccessful startups" will give you the names and business models of failed firms. (Some examples: Anki, Panda TV, Seven Dreamers Laboratory, and Arrivo, There are many others. I hope you have never heard of any of these because if you have, you probably invested in them.) Starting a new business is risky, and many fail, often taking most of the wealth of the founder.

RISK TAKING AND INNOVATION

Why this discussion of risk taking? All these individuals could have had an easier life; each could have remained in a stable job or retired early with a significant amount of wealth. But each decided to continue, often with no certainty of success. All of this happened in a capitalist system.

While there may be many reasons for starting a new business, the most important is usually the chance to make lots of money. In a capitalist system, it is possible to make a lot of money from a new business, as we have seen in considering the richest people in the U.S. But in the socialist world with high taxes and penalties on millionaires and billionaires and little risk capital available, it would be much more difficult or even impossible to become rich through starting a business. We have already seen that socialized medicine alone will greatly increase taxes, and each of Bernie's other entitlements (education, good job, housing, secure retirement, clean environment) will further add to taxes and reduce incentives to undertake risky inventions. Wealth in a socialized economy comes from the government, often through corruption, not from business. Moreover, in a truly socialist economy, the government would take your business if it becomes successful, again reducing incentives.

What does that mean for you? If you are happy with your current devices (phone, laptop, gaming device, home assistant, anything else you own) and the apps you currently use, then the lack of risk taking in a socialist world will apparently not affect you in the future. Actually, many things will not be invented that would have been invented in a freer system, but since they will not be invented, you will not miss them.

We are on the edge of major technological breakthroughs—5G, virtual reality, artificial intelligence, many biomedical possibilities—that will lead to remarkable new apps and devices, and to increased health and an extended lifespan in ways which we can only imagine. A socialist world will remove most of the incentives for inventing and developing these technologies and will slow down the rate of improvement in these and all other products. I believe it would be sad to miss out on the possibilities for future change because a socialist world will reduce the incentives. It will be worse for you than for me because I will not live to see most of these innovations anyway, but you will be missing out on some real benefits.

I don't want to say that there will be no R&D under socialism, but there will be significantly less because incentives will be reduced. Not only will inventions by individual inventors or developers be reduced but also R&D by corporations. Businesses must also make a return on investments in research, and higher taxes to fund socialist programs will also reduce these returns.

Some might counter by arguing that government does the important research, such as the original research for the internet. It is true that some parts of R&D are best done by the government, including research funded by the National Science Foundation or the National Institutes of Health, or sometimes the military through DARPA. Government is good at funding the original basic research. It is not good at commercializing this research to make a viable useful product. NIH funds basic biological research, but when a promising chemical is developed from this research, a private company must do the work to turn the product into a drug and get the product approved and ready for sale.

If we look at Nobel Prizes in the sciences (medicine or physiology, chemistry, physics, economics), we find that the U.S. has more per capita then the European Union, and vastly more than China or Russia. This is because the U.S. is a freer country, and because the tax and incentive system in the U.S. encourages risk taking. For example, the U.S. has more competition between universities, which has led scholars from around the world to move here. You have probably had professors from many different countries, and this is because our education system is more desirable and has better incentives for productivity than any other.

So if we reduce or eliminate the benefits of risk taking, we will reduce willingness to take risks, and this will reduce innovation in the economy.

CHAPTER 9

CAPITALISM, SOCIALISM, AND BUSINESS

You buy products—goods and services—every day. Like most of us, you deal with the markets that exist and don't pay any attention to how these markets came to be. But it will be instructive to examine the history of retail markets under capitalism and to consider how socialism would have affected these markets. More importantly, we can consider the future of retail markets under capitalism and how this future would change under socialism. I discuss retail because all of you are familiar with the workings of this market, but similar stories could be told about any market.

Like me, you probably buy many or most of your products from Amazon. Amazon was founded in 1994 as an online bookstore. As a professor, I read a lot of books, so I was an early adopter of Amazon and later of Amazon Prime. But you as a twenty-year-old person do not remember a world where Amazon did not exist as a major seller of everything. Amazon is only the latest iteration of a long history of retail technologies.

At one time America was a largely rural economy. People made a lot of their own stuff and probably bought what they needed from the local general store. Such a store did not stock much, but people did not buy much. In part this was because people did not have much money, and in part because there were not many things to buy. An early innovation in retail came about from peddlers, people who traveled around the countryside and sold goods to farmers. As you can imagine, there were a limited amount of goods that could be delivered in this way. (The old joke about a salesman for lingerie: "I travel in women's underwear.")

The first major innovation in retailing was the origin of catalog stores, Montgomery Ward in 1872 and Sears Roebuck in 1886. These enterprises took advantage of the new technology of railroads; the First Transcontinental Railroad was completed in about 1869, opening up the possibility of intercontinental trade. Montgomery Ward and Sears (capitalists) took advantage of railroads (built by capitalists) to deliver goods to rural citizens who otherwise would not have had access to a variety of goods and services. Over time, these stores converted to free-standing stores as the benefits of catalog sales declined. Montgomery

Ward ceased operation in 2001, and Sears went bankrupt after a merger with Kmart in 2004.

A simultaneous innovation was the urban department store. One of the modern department stores in the U.S. was Stewart's in New York, which was a successful store by 1848. These stores were successful because the population density of cities meant lots of consumers, and these consumers had enough time and money to shop in large department stores. Later department stores and other stores aggregated into malls because the mobility from automobiles meant that shoppers from a wide area could come to a central location. In the 1960s, discount stores such as Walmart became a large part of the market.

The point of this discussion is not to show nostalgia for the good old days. In fact, we are living in the good new days—online shopping with huge selection and rapid delivery is by far the best method of shopping in history, and we have access to the best selection of goods in history. Rather, the point is twofold. First, it is to show that at any given time there are a few methods of retailing, which can change over time. Although a consumer might assume that whatever methods exist have always been there, in fact distribution systems can radically change. Amazon has not always been there and might not be there forever. The more important point is to show that these changes are driven by the capitalist system. As each type of outlet came into being, each was financed by owners of capital seeking a higher return. (Even though I was an early customer of

Amazon, unfortunately I was too risk averse and not smart enough to be an early investor.) The only way in which such change could occur was if capital was sufficiently mobile to move (perhaps indirectly) from one type of business to another. Investors must be willing to take a chance and hope that they have bet right.

As I write this, we are observing a rapid change in one method of retailing: restaurants. Until recently, the standard way of using a restaurant was to make a reservation (if the restaurant accepted them), go to the restaurant, sit down, and eat. The virus has destroyed that model (hopefully temporarily). Now, a large number of restaurants have begun selling takeout or having food delivered. Some restaurants had always used this model, but it is rapidly becoming universal. Moreover, food delivery services such as DoorDash have grown rapidly to accommodate the change. This all occurred with no central direction, as a market response to market forces.

In a socialist system with central control of capital, such movement may not be possible. For example, in the Soviet Union (before the collapse of communism) consumers would routinely carry a bag in case some desirable good would suddenly become available. When this occurred, a line would quickly form in front of the store so the lucky few in front could buy the desired good before it sold out. Often, consumers would not even know what was being sold; the presence of a line was sufficient information to make waiting worthwhile because it was a signal that the product, whatever it was, was worth buying. Of course, since there were no profits, there was no incentive for more of the good to be produced and no incentive for capital to move into the more productive market.

Aside from the lack of desirable goods, retailing in the Soviet Union was remarkably inefficient. Stores relied on the "three line" system. A consumer would wait in one line to pick out his/her purchase. The clerk would give the consumer a chit indicating what they were buying. The buyer would then take this chit to another line, where they would pay and get a receipt. Then the consumer would take this receipt back to the first line to pick up the goods. This system was quite inefficient in the use of time and could not survive in a competitive market. Of course, because of the inefficiency of production in the system, time was not worth much. (The old joke in the system, which was not actually a joke, was: "We pretend to work, and they pretend to pay us.")

Another socialist inefficiency: In Moscow one would often see people by the side of the road selling (relatively) fresh fruits and vegetables. It turns out that these sellers had flown from the location of the farm to Moscow in order to sell their produce. Although one person flying on a commercial passenger plane to sell only as much produce as they could carry seems a remarkably inefficient method of distribution, the rest of the communist system was so inefficient that this method was still in many cases better than alternatives. (In the U.S. in rural areas one sometimes sees farmers selling their produce by the side of the road, but this is produce they have grown locally, and the method of transportation is the back of a pickup truck, not a passenger airplane. Moreover, only a small percent of output is sold that way.)

In addition to mobility of capital, mobility of labor is also a necessity for change in methods of production. One of Bernie Sanders's points in defining socialism is "the right to a decent job." Although the definition of this is not clear, one possibility is that it becomes difficult to lay workers off—to fire them. For example, as Amazon began to replace conventional retailing, some worried about the jobs lost by retail clerks. Of course, this worry was unfounded—Amazon has hired many warehouse workers. (Those goods don't package and ship themselves.) But if we had Sanders-like laws protecting jobs, then the movement from retail to Amazon might not have happened or might have taken much longer.

You might ask, "So what? Amazon is great, but we already have it. Who needs capital and labor mobility?" Your great-grandparents may have said the same thing about Sears and your grandparents about Walmart and Macy's. Those were good efficient systems for their time, and few would have forecast the rise of Amazon. (Did I mention that I did not buy stock when I began buying books from Amazon?)

Even Amazon is radically changing itself. Many of the goods listed by Amazon are actually sold by others. You can still order from your computer but also from your cell and now from Amazon Echo. There are Amazon retail stores which function with no cash registers or checkout lines. Amazon has its own trucks and no longer contracts with FedEx. Soon there will be Amazon drones. Amazon is also pursuing many other new advanced technologies, though I have no idea what they are. After all, I love my Echo, but I never conceived of it until Amazon told me about it. All of these moves (and similar moves by Google, Walmart, Apple, Facebook and others), require mobility of capital (whether within the firm or from outside) and labor mobility (fewer truck drivers, more drone operators). Amazon is a world seller, again indicating the benefits of the relative freedom to innovate in the U.S. For example, many countries have laws on the books protecting local small businesses from competition, which has hindered the growth and efficiency of their retail sector.

But even though Amazon and the others are busy reinventing themselves to defend against innovations from their existing competitors, that is not the main source of danger to their positions. Rather, the main danger is from two guys in a garage developing technologies that you and I have never heard of and cannot conceive of, just as Walmart never anticipated Amazon, and Amazon did not anticipate Facebook. Maybe it will be an artificial app that tells us what we want before we know it ourselves. Maybe it will be a 3D printer app that will enable us to print stuff and not need to buy it. But it will probably be something that we cannot even envision now. After all, who forecast that a bookstore named after a river and run by a funny-looking bald guy would take over the retail world? (I did not.) Whatever it is, however, we will need capital and labor mobility for it to happen, and a capitalist economy will give us such mobility; a socialist economy will not.

This is the role of "venture capitalists" and other "angels," wealthy individuals or firms who are willing to invest in risky new activities. Such investing is highly risky because many new ventures fail. But this is the process whereby capital moves to new innovations, and a high tax on incomes or wealth would reduce this investing. In a socialist economy there is no possibility of such investing.

Of course, there is a downside to this growth. We can see this downside as we drive through America and observe the empty, closed malls. This is what the great economist Joseph Schumpeter called the process of "creative destruction." If we as a society try too hard to protect the jobs of people in malls or to protect the value of outdated technology, then we will retard this process of growth and innovation. In a socialist economy, the government may own the malls (or whatever technology is becoming outdated) and so pass laws to retard new investment and reduce this innovation. Similarly, if the government tries too hard to protect existing jobs, innovation can be retarded.

Indeed, we should note that whenever a new technology is invented, there are those who claim that it will put existing workers out of work and lead to widespread poverty. The word "sabotage" is named after the noisy wooden shoes of 19th-century French workers who "walked noisily" in labor disputes to retard the growth of machines that were replacing them. (It is commonly thought that workers would throw their wooden shoes into the machines to break them, but Wikipedia indicates that this is incorrect.) The classic folktale and song about John Henry, "a steel driving man" who "died with his hammer in his hand" is about a contest between a human steel driver and a machine used for the same purpose in punching holes for explosives in a mine or, in some versions, railroad track. John Henry won that contest at the cost of his life, and now there are no steel driving men, only machines.

I write this in 2020, when employment was high before the coronavirus attack, and the unemployment rate had been 3.5 percent, a historically low rate. But a few years ago, when unemployment was higher, it was common to read that even high-level jobs would be replaced by computers. Indeed, Socialist Bernie Sanders probably had this period in mind when he said that everyone had the "right to a decent job." Recently (and hopefully again soon) anyone who wanted a job could have had one through the free market. A fundamental principle of economics is that "human wants are insatiable," meaning that there is always something for people to do, and the continued fears of machines putting us out of work are wrong.

In preparing this book, I found a book (on Amazon, of course), *Rise of the Robots: Technology and the Threat of a Jobless Future*, Martin Ford, Basic Books, 2016. In this book Ford argues that, "As technology continues to accelerate and machines begin taking care of themselves, fewer people will be necessary." I don't want to criticize Mr. Ford. He was expressing a common view when his book was written. For example, there are twenty favorable quotes about the book on the inside, from sources such as the *New York Times*, the *Wall Street Journal*, the *Washington Post*, several distinguished economists, and many others, and the book won several prizes. But they were all wrong. Unemployment is now low and falling, and the number of jobs is increasing. We don't need the government to provide "the right to a decent job." The market can handle this by itself if we let it.

In this chapter, I have concentrated on retailing since we all deal with retail markets. But we could tell the same story about any other market. From Marconi's primitive radio to today's 70-inch TVs with surround sound, from Henry Ford's Model T (which was actually itself the product of a long history) to today's 200-mph Ferraris, from the Wright Brothers first airplane to today's supersonic jets, from our ancestor's fire to today's heating and cooling heat pumps, and on and on. And none of these would have been invented in a socialist economy. Indeed, none were.

CHAPTER 10

CAPITALISM, SOCIALISM, AND THE ENVIRONMENT

Capitalism produces more goods than socialism. So you might think that socialism, since it produces less, would use fewer resources and would be better for the environment. A Google search of "socialism and the environment" will find many who have this belief. "...the right to live in a clean environment" is one of the benefits Bernie Sanders promises us from a socialist system, although, like his other benefits, this benefit is not defined, and no method of achieving it is given on his website. The "Green New Deal" also links socialism with a clean environment.

A clean environment is what economists call a "normal good." A normal good is a good whose consumption increases as wealth and incomes increase, at least above some point. That is, a good that people consume more of as they become richer. Since capitalism makes people richer, they prefer an improved environment relative to people living under socialism, which makes people poorer. Moreover, since capitalism is associated with freedom and democracy, governments are likely to be more responsive to citizens' preferences under capitalism.

There are other aspects of capitalism associated with an improved environment.

PROPERTY RIGHTS

One of the most important sources of the difference between property rights in capitalism and socialism. Under capitalism, property rights are clear and well defined for most goods. That is, it is clear who owns something, and the rights to ownership are enforced by law. For example, if you dump trash on my land, I can have you arrested and force you to clean it up. (See the Arlo Guthrie song, "Alice's Restaurant Massacree." You can listen on your Echo or other devices. I strongly recommend it.) In an advanced capitalist economy, all land is owned. If you want to create a landfill, you must purchase the land from the owner and obtain a permit from the relevant government (city, county, or state) before you can build your landfill. You must also follow various regulations that control the way in which you use the landfill. (In a capitalist economy, some regulations are still necessary, and the most important of those regulate environment for reasons I discuss later.)

In a socialist economy, property rights are often not well defined, and individuals do not own private property. While in theory "everyone" owns property in common, in practice this means that either the government owns property, or no one owns it. Even if the government owns the right, government may often be more concerned with output than with protecting property. For example, consider the Aral Sea between Kazakhstan and Uzbekistan in the former Soviet Union. This was at one time the fourth-largest body of inland water in the world. However, the planners in the Soviet Union were more concerned with cotton production than with the health of the lake, and so ended up draining at least half of this lake. Some have called this one of the world's greatest environmental disasters.

One example of inefficient ownership is what is called "the tragedy of the commons." The simple story is this: A piece of land is owned in common by residents of the city. It is common in the sense that anyone in the community is able to graze cows on the land. Let there be one hundred residents, each with one cow, and each cow gives one thousand pounds of meat per year, for a total output of one hundred thousand pounds per year. Now let one farmer (call him Old MacDonald) add an extra cow. Because there is an extra cow, output per cow falls from one thousand pounds per year to 990 pounds per year. Total output falls from one hundred thousand total pounds per year to 99,990 pounds per year. But Old MacDonald has two cows, each producing 990 pounds per year, for a total of 1,980 pounds, an increase (for him) of 980 pounds. Thus, although total output has decreased for all one hundred farmers, Old MacDonald has gained 980 pounds, so adding a cow is a rational decision for him.

But what is rational for Old MacDonald is actually rational for each farmer (Farmer Brown, Farmer Green…). Each time a farmer adds a cow, total output falls more, but private output for the farmer adding a cow can increase, and eventually the land is a swampy mess with a lot of scrawny cows and very little output. In fact, this is exactly what happened to the Boston Common, originally a grazing area in the center of Boston. This area was made into a park exactly because of the commons problem.

This problem is more frequent than it might appear. For example, the same problem applies to fishing rights, where there is a problem of overfishing (from the human perspective; from the fish perspective, any fishing is overfishing). The problem can lead to too many fishing boats and fewer total fish than if there were a better definition of property rights. It can also apply to certain oil rights structures. The reasons such problems are not more common is because capitalism generally solves this problem by defining and enforcing property rights. The property rights owner then has an incentive to enforce the rights. The problem is very common in socialist regimes because there is no property rights owner with an incentive to enforce the rights.

Another area where capitalism is better than socialism is in the use of natural resources, such as steel or aluminum. In a capitalist system, producers are concerned with profits. Using more steel in production is a cost—someone must pay for the steel. Because capitalists want to maximize profits, they will find ways to use as little steel and other raw materials as possible. Socialists are concerned with other goals, such as maximizing output, or whatever goal the State sets for them, which is generally not profits. Therefore, there is little or no incentive to conserve resources, and production is wasteful. When I visited the Soviet Union, I purchased a monocular (one of the few things besides nesting dolls that might have been worth buying). It worked pretty well, and I still use it from time to time, but it was vastly heavier than a similar product made in America.

The soviet economy engaged in excessive logging, leading to deforestation. Again, this is due to lack of efficient property rights. In the U.S. forests are owned, and there is little or no excessive logging.

POLLUTION

A problem common to all systems is air and water pollution. This is because no one owns the air or water—property rights are not well defined. Essentially, pollution is a commons problem. But even though the same problems exist in a capitalist and a socialist system, solutions are very different.

The Soviet Union did a remarkably poor job of protecting the environment. Water was highly polluted—75 percent of surface water and 50 percent of all water was highly polluted. Only 8 percent of wastewater was treated, leading to disease outbreaks such as cholera. Air in industrial centers was highly polluted.

In the U.S. beginning in 1970, the Environmental Protection Agency (EPA) began to protect the environment, including air and water. Although the agency is not perfect, overall, it has done more good than harm—that is, overall, the EPA passes a cost-benefit test. Because of property rights, the U.S. was never as polluted as the Soviet Union, and the EPA has greatly reduced pollution.

There are several reasons for the greater success in the U.S. than in the Soviet Union. First, the U.S. was richer. Environmental cleanliness is expensive, and income in the United States is and was higher. For example, there were many laws in the Soviet Union protecting forests and species. However, in general the staff needed to enforce these laws was not created or funded. In the U.S., similar laws are enforced.

Second, those in charge of the Soviet Union were more concerned with industrial and military progress than with environmental cleanliness. Thus, even if they could have afforded the cost of environmentalism, they were not willing to spend the money needed—they preferred to spend it on other things.

Third, as discussed several times in this book, the Soviet Union was a top down system. Citizens were not happy with dirty air and water, and the disease that resulted, but they had no way to translate these preferences into policy. As a functioning democracy, if enough U.S. voters care about some issue, the government is forced to respond. There is no particular evidence that President Nixon was himself an environmentalist, but he still signed the law creating the EPA because it was necessary for his reelection.

NUCLEAR POWER

Nuclear power is the cleanest and least polluting source of energy. It is greatly underused everywhere. Russia relies on nuclear power for about 21 percent of all its energy and is building more plants. The U.S. is the world's largest producer of nuclear electricity. Nonetheless, we should use it much more than we do if we are worried about the environment. Nuclear power is non-polluting and much safer than any other source of power. It requires little land, unlike wind and solar farms, which take up huge amounts of space and kill birds in addition (chopping by wind or frying by solar).

In 1986, the Russians suffered a major nuclear disaster at the Chernobyl plant when the nuclear plant core over-heated and exploded. About one hundred thousand people were evacuated, and an area of a 19-mile radius was contaminated. It is estimated that the accident caused between nine thousand and fifteen thousand fatalities when all radiation-related deaths are counted in the Soviet Union and in Europe. There were also tremendous expenses associated with the cleanup. Several reactors of the Chernobyl type are still functioning in Russia and may still be dangerous. Because of this disaster, many are opposed to construction of additional nuclear reactors, even though nuclear power is the safest and least polluting source of energy.

Chernobyl is sometimes compared with Three Mile Island, a nuclear accident in Pennsylvania in 1979. However, there were no deaths from Three Mile Island, and cleanup costs were virtually negligible. Nonetheless, many used the combination of Chernobyl and Three Mile Island accidents to argue against nuclear power. But the main lesson from Chernobyl vs. Three Mile Island is that Socialists are less careful than capitalists in building nuclear plants, and probably anything else.

The lesson of this chapter is that although Bernie Sanders calls for the "right to live in a clean environment," socialism has a much poorer record of environmental cleanliness than does capitalism. Under socialism you will have less civil freedom and probably a shorter life expectancy.

CHAPTER 11

MILITARY SERVICE

You may have heard your parents or grandparents discussing the horrors of the Vietnam War draft. This was a method of obtaining soldiers used in the U.S. mainly in wartime. (Listen to the second half of the song "Alice's Restaurant Massacree" by Arlo Guthrie.) It was highly inefficient, since there was no attempt to choose the most efficient set of soldiers—those qualified men (women were not drafted) who would have been willing to serve for the lowest wage. The draft ended in 1972. Technically, men are still required to register for the draft, but the law does not seem to be enforced, and no one has been conscripted (drafted) since 1972. During the Vietnam War, there was widespread opposition to the draft with many protests and riots, and many taking extreme steps to avoid military service, including even emigration to Canada.

Since 1973 we have relied on a "volunteer army." (This is an odd phrase since we rely on "volunteer teachers," "volunteer waiters," and indeed volunteers for every position in the country but refer only to the military as "volunteer.") But the bottom line is that if you live in the U.S., unless there is a major war, you will not be conscripted to serve in the military. (Given modern military technology, if there is a major war it will probably be over before there is a chance to draft you.) You may of course choose to join the military, and pay and benefits have been increased to the level where enough individuals join, as in any other occupation in a free society.

The Soviet Union and Russia have always had a draft, even in peacetime. Moreover, military conditions have been quite unpleasant for draftees. For example, in Russia the term of service was at one time two years. However, second-year draftees treated first-year draftees so badly, sometimes even beating them to death, that the term was reduced to eighteen months.

There is an additional effect of a conscripted military: death rates in a conscripted military are higher than in a volunteer military. This may be because volunteers stay in the military longer and so are better trained, or it may be because volunteers are more expensive and so more is spent by the military on preserving lives. It may also be because every time a soldier is killed, potential enlistees are deterred, and so wages must increase, adding to military costs.

In the table below, I consider deaths per year in two conscripted militaries, the U.S. in Vietnam and the Soviet army in Afghanistan with the U.S. army in Afghanistan and in Iraq.

Conflict	Length	Number of deaths	Deaths per year
U.S. Vietnam (Conscript)	12 years, 1963-1975 (Years of significant involvement)	58,318	4,859
USSR Afghanistan (Conscript)	10 Years (1979-1989)	14,453	1,445
U.S. Afghanistan (Volunteer)	19 Years (2001-present)	2,419	127
U.S. Iraq (Volunteer)	7 years (2003-2009) (Main U.S. involvement)	4,496	642

Source: Constructed by author from Wikipedia entries for each war.

The lesson from this table is clear. There are many fewer deaths per year for a volunteer army than for a conscripted army. This applies both to U.S. wars over time and to wars in Afghanistan with either conscripts (USSR) or volunteers (U.S.). The large number of deaths and the involuntary nature of those chosen (conscripted) for the military explains why the Vietnam War was so unpopular. Conversely, the relatively small number of deaths in Afghanistan and Iraq, and the fact that the military was made up of volunteers, may explain the relative lack of political opposition to the more recent wars. Our wars are now more expensive, but an increase in taxation does not seem to draw the same protests as a draft.

So you are more likely to be conscripted for military service in a socialist state than in a capitalist state, and if you are conscripted, you are more likely to die.

CHAPTER 12

WORST CASE SCENARIO

In this chapter, I discuss the deaths caused by communism. I thought a lot about including this chapter because I don't want to be accused of being an alarmist. *I don't want to imply that if we adopted the form of socialism advocated by Bernie Sanders and his followers there will be massive deaths in the U.S.*

On the other hand, I think it is important to understand exactly what communism meant for the countries adopting it. For example, Wikipedia defines communism as: "In political and social sciences, communism (from Latin *communis*, "common, universal") is the philosophical, social, political, and economic ideology and movement whose ultimate goal is the establishment of the communist society, which is a socioeconomic order structured upon the common ownership of the means of production and the absence of social classes, money, and the state."

While communism is a philosophical ideology that sounds very nice, and this may be what you learned in school if you studied communism at all, it has also been a brutal method of governing, resulting in more than 94 million deaths, according to the *Black Book of Communism.* This is a book written by several European scholars and published in the U.S. by Harvard University Press. It is the standard source for documenting communism's crimes. By contrast, the Nazis killed about 21 million people.

Deaths from Communism, by Country (*Black Book of Communism*):

- 65 million in the People's Republic of China
- 20 million in the Soviet Union
- 2 million in Cambodia
- 2 million in North Korea
- 1.7 million in Ethiopia
- 1.5 million in Afghanistan
- 1 million in the Eastern Bloc
- 1 million in Vietnam
- 150,000 in Latin America
- 10,000 deaths "resulting from actions of the international Communist movement and Communist parties not in power"

Many of these deaths were from intentional starvation, although many were from more active methods.

Socialism does not have the same record, although Venezuela may be in the process of creating record, mainly from starvation. Socialism does lead to deaths from reduced incomes and perhaps inefficient farming and poor medicine, but no socialist state has set out to murder its citizens. Nonetheless, since socialist states sometimes become communist, it is at least worth understanding the danger of movements in that direction.

CHAPTER 13

SUMMARY OF PART I: ALL YOU REALLY NEED TO KNOW

If you are willing to believe me, then all you really need to know is in Part I and in this summary.

Socialism will reduce your income. Part of this will be the taxes required to pay for socialistic programs. Part will be that these higher taxes will reduce incentives for work, and so will reduce GDP. It is not possible to pay for the programs proposed by the socialists with taxes on the rich; taxes on the middle class must also increase.

Under socialism, government programs will replace private programs. What has best been studied and what is proposed by contemporary socialists for the U.S. is the health care system. Current plans proposed by socialists such as Bernie Sanders would totally eliminate all private health insurance, including employer provided insurance, and would forbid anyone from purchasing any health insurance that was not part of the government plan. Everyone would have the same health insurance plan and the same medical care; it would be a "one size fits all" plan. Because government health insurance would add patients and coverage but would not increase (and would probably decrease) the number of doctors, everyone would have a relatively low-quality plan.

Some people are richer than others. In a market economy, the only legal way to get rich is to produce something that others are willing to pay for—that is, the only way to get rich is to provide goods and services to others that they value. We examined the ten richest people in the country and found that all of them did indeed produce something of value. Under a socialist system, some are richer or more powerful than others, but this does not imply that they provided anything of value. They are probably just more capable of exploiting people.

By increasing taxes on the rich ("millionaires and billionaires") and by generally reducing incomes, socialism will reduce incentives for invention. We live in a world where many of the things we rely on in our day-to-day lives (computers, cell phones, Amazon, Facebook, Apple, Google) are new and where new things are continually being created. Virtual reality, 5G, artificial intelligence, and biomedical innovation are all about to generate a host of new inventions that will influence our lives in ways we cannot even imagine. Socialism will greatly retard the rate of development of these new technologies.

Socialism may increase your chances of being drafted into the military and of being killed if you are drafted.

Finally, socialism will reduce your freedom. At the least, it will reduce our economic freedom, your freedom to spend your money. It is possible that socialism might reduce your freedom even more, At worst, almost all freedom could be eliminated.

I promised that we would not discuss theory or other countries' experience with socialism. So far, I have tried to keep that promise, and if all you are concerned with is the effect of socialism on your lives, you can stop reading now. If you are curious, you can continue. Part II strengthens the argument of Part I. In the next chapter I discuss some evidence about socialism, and then I discuss why it is that some people prefer socialism. Finally, I discuss capitalism and show the important ways in which it differs from socialism.

PART II

IF YOU ARE STILL CURIOUS

CHAPTER 14

HOW HAS SOCIALISM WORKED?

THE GREATEST ECONOMIC EXPERIMENT IN HUMAN HISTORY

The greatest economic or social science experiment in history lasted from the Russian Revolution in 1917, until the dissolution of the Soviet Union in 1991 During this time the USSR basically competed with the U.S. during the Cold War. The issue raised by the conflict was the relative strength of a government run, centrally planned, top down command economy or a bottom up free market economy. Many economists had long known that a command economy could not compete, but it took the actual collapse of the Soviet Union to provide convincing evidence to everyone (except for a few hardcore Marxists, including Bernie). Moreover, the Soviet Union concentrated its production on military goods and still could not compete militarily with the United States, which made mainly civilian goods and still out competed the Soviet Union in military production.

"Socialism" is part of a continuum of government involvement in the economy. Every country has some government involvement, if only to protect property rights, enforce contracts, protect the public health, and provide defense—a minimal libertarian government. Government needs to collect some taxes to fund these activities. (All governments actually do more than this.) At the other extreme, in a pure socialist, or communist, economy, government does virtually everything and owns all the means of production. If we define socialism as government control of the means of production, *then no socialist country has ever been successful.*

The closest thing to a pure socialist economy was the Soviet Union. While there were various forms of central control which changed over time, all of them basically involved government control of the economy and various "five-year plans" which were the mechanism used to control the economy. This included an effort to control both production processes and prices as well as quantities of all goods. The economy was aimed mainly at producing military goods and capital goods rather than consumer goods.

As discussed at various places in this book, a centrally controlled economy is highly inefficient as compared with a capitalist economy. It is impossible for a centrally planned system to understand what goods and services should be produced, what technology should be used for production, or what price each good should sell for. The Soviet economy was further hampered by a belief in Marxism, which was a fundamentally flawed view of the world. For example, Marx argued that larger factories were more productive than smaller factories. (This was part of his view of monopoly capitalism: he believed that capitalism would degenerate into a series of monopolies.) As a result, the Soviet Union built very large factories—much larger than in the U.S.—and too large to be efficient. In the U.S., markets determined factory size. So when Russia ceased to be run as a communist society, most of the factories shut down or greatly downsized because they were inefficiently large and could not survive without government subsidies.

Government run factories were also in charge of military goods. The USSR spent about 40 percent of its GDP on defense (while the U.S. spent about 5 percent). As a result, when the U.S. began researching anti-missile technologies ("Star Wars," the Strategic Defense Initiative) under President Reagan, the Russians could not keep up. Realizing that the Soviet economy was stretched to the limit, President Gorbachev, the final leader of the Soviet Union, began to loosen up, hoping to become economically more efficient. This effort basically failed, and ultimately the economy collapsed, followed by the collapse of the USSR.

Another example: For some reason, Stalin became a believer in Lysenkoism, a flawed biological theory that claimed that acquired characteristics of a plant or animal could be inherited. What Stalin believed, everyone who was not in Siberia believed. As a result, many biologists were arrested or exiled. This theory, which is inconsistent with Darwinism and is clearly wrong, was nonetheless applied to Soviet agriculture with highly detrimental results. This, along with the collectivization of Soviet farms, was one of the reasons for massive famines in the Soviet Union and millions of deaths from starvation. The Soviets claimed the cause was bad weather, but bad weather can only last so long.

We should also note that Russians were much poorer than Americans. Although official statistics did not reflect this poverty because the official exchange rate was one ruble per dollar, the actual rate was more like seven rubles per dollar, as I learned when I visited the Soviet Union. Of course, the Soviets were more concerned with industrial and military production than with consumer goods, an example of top down control.

So the Soviet Union was a very inefficient economy and eventually collapsed. Some other implications of its inefficiency: While it was operating, information was greatly restricted. For example, when the U.S. was shown on TV, only the most unfavorable news—crimes, civil right protests—was shown. Books and magazines about the U.S. were greatly restricted. Also, emigration from the country (for example, Jews wanting to go to Israel) was restricted. Under Lenin and Stalin, many crimes were punishable by exile to Siberia or death. Things were less draconian later but still quite severe. Walking the streets of Moscow in 1981, my wife and I were impressed (negatively) by the silence on the streets—no one was talking. On a later visit, after the collapse of the Soviet Union, the streets were much more normal, and people were dressed much better.

CAPITALISM VERSUS SOCIALISM

The beauty of a capitalist system, as first shown by Adam Smith in his great book, *Wealth of Nations,* is that an economy can run based on private self-interested decisions which work, according to Smith, as an "invisible hand." ("…directing that industry in such a manner as its produce may be of the greatest value, he intends only his own gain, and he is in this, as in many other cases, led by an invisible hand to promote an end which was no part of his intention." Adam Smith, *Wealth of Nations*, 1776.) As the government controls more of an economy, this self-directing mechanism becomes lost, and an economy must rely more and more on central control and central planning. There are many problems with central planning.

The two most important are information problems and incentive problems.

Consider information. A market economy is extremely efficient in its use of information. Think of kale. For reasons that escape me, in recent years consumers have begun to desire kale—what economists call a change in tastes. What happens? Grocery stores begin to observe that whatever kale they carried was sold out quickly. The grocer does not need to know why this happened; all he needs to observe is that the kale is selling more quickly. This leads to two responses. First, he will raise the price of kale. Second, he will tell his supplier that he wants to order more kale and is willing to pay more for it. The supplier in turn notices that the price at which she can sell kale is increasing, and so she orders more kale from the farmers who sell to her, again offering a higher price. Farmers will in turn grow more kale, and next season there will be more kale available in the grocery stores.

Notice that no one needs to understand why the demand for kale has increased. (I still find it a puzzle.) All the grocer needs to know is that he can sell his kale for a higher price and similarly for each step all the way back to the farmer. The market process does not require that anyone understands the entire process; each party need only know what is happening to the price at which he or she can sell the product. Also, no one needs to tell anyone what to do. Each party responds to its own incentives— each wants to make money; the self-interest of each party leads to the market responding to the increased demand for kale. This is the invisible hand at work. Consumers want more kale and they get it, with no one ordering that it happen.

Now consider a centrally planned economy. Prices are controlled, so the increased demand for kale will not lead to a price increase. Thus, the grocer sells out of kale, but this does not lead to a price increase, so the supplier has no way of knowing that there has been an increase in demand. And even if he does know, he has no incentive to stock more since he does not own his store, and no one has any interest in increasing the store's profits. There is no mechanism for translating increased consumer demand to increased amount available. This is why the former Soviet Union continually suffered shortages and why it ultimately collapsed.

Think of the information needed to plan an economy. There are millions of consumers, each with his or her own set of preferences. There are millions of enterprises, each with its own set of technologies and inputs. To come up with a viable central plan which coordinates consumer demand with producer supply, someone would need to know all the information about each person's preferences and about the technologies available to each firm. But of course, no one can. The market—the invisible hand—can aggregate all this information in a truly remarkable way. We in a market system take the functioning of the market for granted (when we go to the store we can buy what we want, and we don't even think about the complex processes that made this possible), but if we eliminate this mechanism in favor of socialist central planning, we would quickly come to appreciate what we would have given up.

The second issue is incentives. Even if the central planner had the information needed to satisfy consumer demands, he would have no incentive to do so. This is because there are no profits in a communist or fully socialist economy, and without profits there are no incentives to do things well. A story is told of the manager of a furniture factory in the Soviet Union. He was told that his compensation depended on the number of chairs that the factory produced. So the factory produced thousands of chairs, but each was too flimsy to use. He was then told that he would be rewarded based on the weight of the furniture he produced. Result? A small number of chairs so massive that no one could move them. I don't know if this particular story is true, but it does illustrate the difficulty of controlling production with no profit signal to guide managers. In a market economy, the manager would respond to market prices and would produce those chairs whose combination of weight, price, and style would maximize his profits. If he made a mistake and produced the wrong chairs, some competitor would produce the right ones, and the wrong chairs would be sold in a distress sale, perhaps on Overstock.com. Even if the Soviet manager tried to maximize profits based on current prices, there is no reason for him to get things right since in a command economy prices are arbitrary and not determined by the market.

When I visited the Soviet Union and found that the exchange rate on the street was about 7 rubles per dollar. I was excited: I could buy cheap rubles and buy lots of stuff at a steep discount. But I quickly learned that there was nothing I wanted to buy except little dolls that fit one inside another, a product with little use, except as a souvenir. There was some innovation even in this market: the original version of "matryoshka" dolls was women or girls decreasing in size. Later versions had Lenin, Stalin, Malenkov, Khrushchev, Brezhnev, Andropov, Chernenko down to Gorbachev or Yeltsin, and now I suppose Putin. While this was an innovation, it was not one that increased human welfare or GDP by much. The inefficiency of the Soviet economy was such that even at an 84 percent discount, there was virtually nothing worth buying.

Even the food in restaurants was no good. Although we don't eat at McDonald's much in the U.S., in the USSR we ate there whenever it was convenient because the food at McDonald's was better than most of the food we could find, even in quality restaurants. In fact, it took some time for McDonald's to open in Russia because McDonald's needed to teach the Russian farmers how to grow meat and potatoes of sufficient quality.

EVIDENCE

This is the theory. The evidence is also consistent with this theory. Consider the socialist or communist countries of the 20th and 21st centuries—the Soviet Union and its satellites or imitators: East Germany, North Korea, Cuba, Maoist China, Venezuela, Zimbabwe. Some countries at one time had much larger government sectors, more or less consistent with socialism: the Nordic countries, Great Britain, India, and Israel. As I discussed above, the Soviet Union collapsed, and many of the countries in the "Union" have separated from Russia, which is still trying to recover from its eighty years of communism, although it is now much more prosperous than it was under communism. Some countries of the former Soviet Union (Georgia, Ukraine, Moldova, Belarus, Armenia, Estonia, Latvia, Lithuania, Azerbaijan, Kazakhstan, Uzbekistan, Turkmenistan, Kyrgyzstan, Tajikistan) and its satellites (Poland, the Czech Republic, Hungary, Slovenia, Romania, East Germany, Albania, and Yugoslavia now that it has ended its civil wars) are doing much better now that they are no longer forced to be communist, but some have retained Soviet-era type governments and are doing poorly.

East Germany and North Korea are themselves each case studies. Capitalist West Germany was vastly more successful and richer than Communist East Germany (so much so that a wall was needed to keep people from leaving the east), and it was only after the countries were reunited under control of the capitalist west that the east began to grow. South Korea is a very productive country and makes a lot of stuff that we happily buy. North Korea is the least successful country in the world. In both Korea and Germany, the people and pre-communist cultures were the same, but the difference was the economic system. South Korea and West Germany were capitalist systems; North Korea and East Germany were communist.

Cuba was much richer as a capitalist country and it made good cigars, even though it was a dictatorship. As a socialist country, it is now poorer, and I am told even the cigars are no good. China has become richer since giving up its extreme Maoist communist system, which caused many millions of deaths from starvation. China on a per capita basis is still much poorer than the U.S. It still has too many remnants of communism left to become a really rich country. It is also not a democratic country, and it is run as a dictatorship. Zimbabwe was ruled for thirty-seven years by Robert Mugabe, a brutal dictator and a firm Marxist. In 2000, Mugabe instituted a policy of "land reform" which essentially destroyed the property rights of white farmers in the country. This led to a complete economic collapse as banks failed and foreign investors refused to invest in the chaotic country.

The Berlin Wall and other impediments to emigration show something important about communism. The purpose of these walls was to keep people *in*, not to keep them out. Virtually all communist countries have made it difficult or impossible to leave. This is because residents can see that their non-communist neighbors are much wealthier. At the Berlin Wall, for example, guards were trained to shoot potential defectors, and even so there were still those who attempted to leave. An exception is Venezuela, where people are allowed to leave and are doing so in droves. Whether this will remain the case is an open question. Capitalist countries often make efforts to control borders, but they are concerned with keeping people *out*, not *in*.

Great Britain, the Nordic countries, India, and Israel have greatly reduced the size of government and have become much more prosperous as a result. These countries found life under socialism or excessive government unacceptable, and so democratically reduced the government sector. These countries were examples of "democratic socialism," but the democratic aspect resulted in eliminating socialism. Bernie Sanders is an advocate of "democratic socialism," but it seems inefficient to elect a socialist government only so that we can later get rid of it. Moreover, during the time of the socialist government, lives are worse, people are poorer, and the economic growth that is lost during the socialist period can never be recovered.

Now consider Venezuela, the most recent example of socialism. Venezuela has large oil reserves and was at one time the richest country in Latin America. In 1999, Hugo Chavez nationalized the oil industry and began a process of nationalization of industries, price controls, and increased taxes. Chavez was democratically elected, so the socialism of Venezuela meets one definition of "democratic socialism." In 2011, the "Law of Fair Costs and Prices" (which sounds like a satirical name for a fictional government law invented by free market novelist Ayn Rand) gave an agency the power to control prices and costs. It is possible for government to control prices, but it is not possible to control costs, so most products had costs increase above prices, and so were no longer worth producing. There have been shortages of aspirin, food, toilet paper, and most other goods.

Nicolás Maduro became president in 2013 and continued these policies. As of 2019, Venezuela was a total basket case, and people have been leaving as fast as they can. There was also inflation approaching the level of 1,000,000 percent per year. Recently, however, Venezuela has reduced its socialist policies. Venezuelans are using dollars as currency, and the bolivar is virtually worthless and not in use. Moreover, the government has greatly reduced regulation and has allowed private investment. As a result, the Venezuelan economy has greatly improved. Many Venezuelans had dollars invested in the U.S. but previously were not allowed to repatriate or use these dollars. Since the government has relaxed currency controls, Venezuelans have begun repatriating their dollars, and living standards have significantly increased.

Note that the collapse happened in less than twenty years. Venezuela went from a prosperous country to a total basket case in a very short period of time after adopting socialist policies. In the first part of this book I described some of the likely implications of socialism for the U.S., but the story of Venezuela indicates that things could easily be worse even than I predicted and could happen faster. However, just as it was surprising how quickly the economy collapsed under socialism, it is also surprising how quickly it seems to be recovering as socialism has been relaxed.

The U.S. press seems to avoid true discussions of the evils of socialism. When you read about Venezuela in the press, the stories often do not mention socialism. A Google search of "causes of Venezuela collapse" leads to 5,820,000 articles; if we add "socialism," the number falls to 2,170,000 articles. In other words, less than half of the articles discussing the cause of the Venezuelan collapse mention the true cause, socialism. This may be part of the reason so many do not understand the true costs of socialism. Articles often mention "other causes" such as poor management of the oil industry. But as discussed earlier in this book, poor management is a natural feature of socialism since there are no incentives for good management, and the information conveyed by market prices is missing.

It is sometimes argued that the Nordic countries (Sweden, Norway, Denmark, Iceland, and Finland) are the model for the success of democratic socialism. There are two problems with this argument. First, there is no

IF YOU ARE STILL CURIOUS

sense in which these countries are socialist. They have free markets, and in some senses are less regulated than the U.S. has been. The government does not control the means of production; there are private firms and private property. (The U.S. has become less regulated under the deregulation policies of the Trump administration except for international trade, so the comparison needs to be updated.) These countries have universal health insurance, but they do not have a single-payer system and, unlike the proposal for Medicare for All, they have significant co-pays and competition to limit overuse of the medical system and to control costs.

Second, these countries have incomes about 15 percent lower than in the U.S., so they cannot be viewed as being as economically successful. It is interesting that people of Nordic ancestry have significantly higher incomes (20-30 percent higher) in the U.S. than in the Nordic countries.

The Nordic countries have higher taxes in some sectors than the U.S., although lower in others, but overall taxes (federal, state, and local) are about 50 percent of GDP, as compared with 38 percent in the U.S. Indeed, these countries have reduced their tax rates by 20-30 percent since the 1970s and 1980s because the higher tax rates were stifling economic growth. Perhaps Mr. Sanders is still viewing them as they were when he first learned about these countries and socialism.

Taxation in Scandinavian countries is less progressive than in the U.S. The highest marginal rate in the U.S.

is 41 percent on incomes above $600,000; in Denmark the highest rate is 56 percent on incomes over $80,000. Moreover, these countries have a value added tax (essentially, a sales tax) which is largely paid by the middle class. As I argued earlier, the only way to finance a large welfare state is through taxes on the middle class. There are other complex differences between taxation in the Nordic countries and the U.S.

It is not correct to call these countries socialist, and it is still true that no socialist country has been an economic success. The only "democratic socialist" countries have actually used the democratic nature of the government to reject the socialistic part.

CHAPTER 15

WHY SOCIALISM?

If socialism and its cousins have been such a disaster whenever they have been tried, why do so many in the U.S. and elsewhere support socialism, as shown in many recent polls and by the performance of Bernie Sanders and other candidates in various polls and elections? One possibility is that many do not understand exactly what is meant by socialism. Indeed, one purpose of this book is to show what socialism means. However, Mr. Sanders has been preaching socialism for many years (he is seventy-seven years old and has been a socialist most of his adult life). He clearly knows what he is proposing. Others in his camp also understand the implications. Mr. Sanders says he is advocating "democratic socialism," but no one knows what that means, unless it means the ability to get rid of socialism when it leads to poverty and unrest. As mentioned above, Venezuela initially elected a socialist government, so in that sense, Venezuela is a democratic socialist country, but the government has rigged elections so that it has been impossible to change its government. (One person, one vote, one time.) The Nordic countries are democratic but not socialist. They voted for governments that reduced the size of government, as did India, Israel, and Great Britain.

Few if any countries have voluntarily chosen socialism. Communism in Russia was imposed after a revolution, and the socialist republics and satellite countries were forcibly converted after World War II, as was North Korea. Cuba was socialist because of the Castro revolution. China became communist after a long civil war following World War II. Venezuela did elect Hugo Chavez but is unable to get rid of his successor. I write this in 2020. Should we elect a socialist in the 2020 election, we will be one of the few countries to voluntarily choose socialism.

As I write this in winter 2020, there are major riots in Hong Kong. The people of Hong Kong want to be free of communist domination, and China is trying to maintain or increase its control. When you read this, you will probably know how the story ends. But the conflict tells something about socialism: intelligent people resist socialism. Those with power in a socialist country try to maintain their power. We can tell a similar story for Venezuela, and for many other socialist countries, including Hungary in 1956 (against Russian control) and the collapse of the Soviet Union itself. When given the chance, people vote against socialism. If voting becomes impossible, people will try to use other means, including violence, to eliminate socialism.

One reason why some prefer socialism is a deep misunderstanding of a market economy. Think of our economy. There are about 160 million people in the labor force. The total population is about 327 million. There are about 30 million businesses in the U.S. Amazon does not sell all products available in the U.S., but it does sell 560 million products, and this of course does not include services. Think of what this means: 160 million people organized in 30 million businesses selling more than 560 million separate products to 327 million consumers. How can that be?

One's first thought is that this would lead to chaos. No one is in charge! How do we organize this mass of stuff? A first thought is that the system would not work, and we must put someone in charge, or the entire thing will lead to chaos and collapse. That first thought is the impetus for defending socialism or central planning. We must put someone in charge! Anyway, who decided that there should be 560 million separate products? That is clearly too many. We could easily get by with many fewer products—say, one brand of each good.

In fact, think of it in reverse. The number of people and products means that no central planner could have the knowledge to coordinate all of their myriad plans and preferences. Rather, the opposite is true: the only way for the system to work is for each person or firm to make their own decisions. Each entity knows what it wants and what it can do. Consumers know their own preferences (what economists call a "utility function") and producers know their own technology ("production function"). This is the beauty of the decentralized market: it allows decisions to be made at the level of information.

In fact, economists have known since about 1776 (when Adam Smith published *Wealth of Nations*, the beginning of modern economics) that you don't actually need anyone in charge. It is one of the most remarkable results in all of science, but a free market economy directed by self-interest and profit-seeking individuals can actually obtain efficient and consistent results and will not crash into chaos. While proofs of this result can become quite technical, the simple model of supply and demand and the invisible hand takes us a fair way towards understanding the equilibrium in an economy.

Consider a price—say, the price of bread. (Ignore the fact that there are many types of bread. I prefer rye.) This price must perform many functions. First, it must equate supply and demand in the bread market. But a consumer's demand for bread depends on her income and on the prices of all other goods—butter, peanut butter, salami, turkey, cheese, potato chips. The price of bread must make purchases of bread consistent with all of these other prices.

Consider the supply side. The price of bread must be high enough to generate the wheat (or rye) that is used to produce the flour that goes into the bread. The price of wheat must be high enough to pay for the labor of the farmers who grow the wheat, and to pay for the fertilizer and pesticides and tractors that are used to grow the wheat, and to pay for the land that is used to grow wheat instead of the next best alternative (the "opportunity cost" of the land). The price must also be used to pay for the processing of the wheat into flour, the flour into bread, the packaging, the transportation, the retail cost.

What is truly amazing is that all of these prices are consistent with each other. The price that compensates the resources needed to produce the bread is also the price that leads the consumers to purchase the amount of bread that suppliers choose to produce and also the price that leads consumers to purchase the right amount of peanut butter and jelly to go on the bread. All of the prices in a free economy are consistent with each other, and this leads to an equilibrium that has several nice characteristics. This is one of the strongest results in all of science and a result that enables a market economy to function. (To economists, this result is proven in a branch of economics called "general equilibrium theory." Several economists have won Nobel Prizes for results in this area of research.)

So why don't socialists understand this? Fundamentally, because they are mired in a model of the economy which is based on primitive thinking. (Bernie Sanders attended the University of Chicago, but he must have avoided taking any courses from Milton Friedman, a Nobel winning economist at the University of Chicago, and a tremendous defender of the free market.) It is also possible that socialists are control freaks and want additional power to control our lives, perhaps for their view of our benefit, perhaps for theirs, and they are able to take advantage of the ignorance of voters. (If you are a socialist, draw your own conclusions.) As President Reagan said, the scariest words in the English language are, "I'm from the government and I'm here to help you." These words would be even scarier under socialism.

A belief in socialism may also come from a fundamental misunderstanding of economics.

FOLK ECONOMICS

"Folk economics" is the set of economic beliefs of people untrained in economics. One of the tenets of folk economics is that the world is largely zero-sum—economic values do not change in response to changes in prices. I have come to believe that this issue—zero-sum thinking—is responsible for most of the major fallacies in economic policy, such as minimum wages, rent control, and tariffs, all policies that reduce human welfare. Zero-sum thinking leads to emphasis on the "division of the pie" not the "size of the pie," because the size of the pie is viewed as fixed in a world plagued by zero-sum thinking.

One of the fundamental policies of socialism and Marxism is, "From each according to his ability, to each according to his needs." Both halves of this proposal are based on zero-sum thinking. The emphasis on ability ignores the fact that output depends not only on ability but also on incentives. Do I go to college? If so, what do I study? Art appreciation might be more fun than accounting or chemistry or economics (although I enjoyed it), but it does not pay as well. Once I graduate, how hard do I work? How much do I save? Does my spouse work? All of these are subsidiary decisions not based on ability but on incentives. In a zero-sum world, none of this matters; output is fixed and based only on "ability." In the real world in which we live, ours, these things do matter.

Similarly, what are needs? We do not live in a subsistence economy, and each of us gets more than a subsistence amount, so the concept of need is not useful. We all have different preferences, and what we consume depends in part on those preferences. Again, we are not in a zero-sum world or a subsistence world, so consumption is not based on needs but on preferences and prices.

One reason why socialists worry about the wealth of others is because of a deep fallacy in the way they view wealth. The view of Bernie Sanders and his followers that wealth and income are zero-sum for an economy is an important part of folk economics. If the total income of a country (its Gross Domestic Product) is zero-sum—a fixed amount—then as Bill Gates earns more, you must earn less. In a zero-sum world, there would indeed be a pot of income to divide, and more for some would mean less for others. But in the actual non-zero-sum world in which we live, the amount of income for each individual is determined by the decisions of that individual operating in a market, and different decisions can lead to different outcomes. Belief in a zero-sum world is one of the major fallacies leading to destructive economic policies, including socialism.

In particular, economics teaches us that individual earnings are approximately equal to each individual's "marginal product," the additional contribution of a worker to earnings of the employer. This means that as a first approximation, differences in earnings are due to differences in productivity, and those with higher earnings are simply more productive. Moreover, the total product created by an individual (whether a worker or an investor) is greater than the marginal product, so that higher-earning individuals also contribute more to society. By creating Microsoft, Bill Gates and his colleagues (many of whom are also on the Fortune list of the wealthiest individuals in the world) did not take anything from the rest of us. Rather, by creating the computer revolution in the 20th century, these people made our lives so much better that you probably have trouble comprehending a world with no mobile phones, no computers, no email, no Instagram. I lived much of my life in such a world, and I can barely remember it. Each of the individuals who created a major internet company (Google, Microsoft, Apple, Facebook, Amazon, Uber, Airbnb, and many smaller companies) did not take anything from us, even though they are really rich. Rather, they greatly enriched our lives.

Our minds evolved in a simpler world, and they did not evolve to understand a modern economy. All humans growing up in a normal world learn to talk. But we must be taught to read; reading is not part of our natural mental architecture. Economics is like reading: we do not intuitively understand a modern economy.

In the zero-sum world in which our minds evolved, the only way to become rich was to steal from others. There was no technological change and no investment, and so no possibilities of becoming rich by inventing a new stone ax or investing in a growing beaver pelt industry. Therefore, prejudice against the rich is part of our evolved mental architecture. Class conflict (capital versus labor or today's version: race, class, and gender) is also a product of zero-sum thinking—the pie is viewed as fixed, and the only relevant issues are the division of the pie. In fact, of course, labor and capital cooperate to produce output, as do members of different races, classes, and genders, and the amount of output depends on the rules governing use of inputs, such as tax rates.

Another pillar of folk economics is that labor is the only source of value. This was true when our minds were evolving and there was relatively little capital (a few grass huts and stone axes), but it certainly is not true now. But the labor theory of value is part of socialism and part of our untrained primitive thinking. Our minds evolved in a setting with little specialization, trade, or division of labor, all fundamental parts of a modern economy. Folk economics does not understand invisible hand theories of social organization, and so requires central planning. The

Marxist-Sanders theory of exploitation is based on a labor theory of value, where all value is created by labor, and anything that does not go to labor is stolen—exploited—from workers.

While these primitive views are part of our evolved mental structure, it is certainly possible to learn that they are false. (The purpose of this book is to teach you that they are false.) But the modern view of economics is not a natural way of thinking. Consider flat earth thinking: our intuition is that the earth is flat, but we can learn that it is not. Zero-sum thinking is like flat earth thinking. However, it is particularly ironic that those who profess a "deep" understanding of the economy and the advocates of what Marx called "scientific socialism," are actually advocating a primitive, pre-scientific view of the world. Perhaps the best way to counter these views is to point out that they are primitive. Intellectuals do not want to be "on the wrong side of history" nor do they want to be science deniers.

Zero-sum thinking is a pervasive fallacy and leads to many inefficient policies—policies that make you and me worse off. It is easy to understand the source of zero-sum thinking. Many day-to-day events take place in a zero-sum world. If Jack gets the cookie, then Suzie does not. If Judy gets the promotion, then John does not. But in the long term, the world is not zero-sum. Think of how much richer your parents are than your grandparents, or of the world you may have studied in history or anthropology, which was much poorer than today's world. This is not because you or your parents were smarter or luckier or worked harder; it is because of real economic growth and technological change, which have made everyone richer over time.

Economists have indirectly and inadvertently contributed to the negative view of markets—what has been called "emporiophobia," the fear of markets. We characterize the world as being competitive, which is consistent with a zero-sum world, with winners and losers. In fact, the economy is not competitive; it is actually cooperative. The fundamental unit of economics is the exchange, and exchanges are voluntary. Competition is important because competition determines who will engage in exchange and makes sure that exchange takes place on the most favorable terms. But the benefit from an economy is the consumer surplus that is generated by exchange. Cooperation is the movie; competition is the casting director.

GIVING BACK

We often see calls to "give back" by donating to charity. Google indicates that there are 154 million mentions of "giving back." While many of these are self-serving requests for contributions from charities, a sampling of these listings indicates that giving to charity helps create a "purpose" in life. The assumption (sometimes explicit, but always implicit) is that what we do in the workplace to earn our money is somehow selfish, but we can help others by giving to charity.

I have no difficulty with charity; my wife and I donate to several charities. Moreover, someone with the wealth of Bill Gates or Warren Buffett or any of the other multi-billionaires (or even multimillionaires) cannot really spend all their wealth, nor can their descendants. Once one becomes sufficiently wealthy, there is no option but to give money to charity. Moreover, Mr. Gates is apparently doing a commendable job through his foundation of allocating his (and Mr. Buffett's, who has contracted out his charitable giving to Mr. Gates) contributions to the most efficient causes.

Mr. Gates and Mr. Buffett have created the "Giving Pledge," whereby wealthy individuals pledge to give a significant portion of their wealth to charity. Overall, 204 individuals or families have signed this pledge, including, in addition to Mr. Gates and Mr. Buffett, others from our list of ten: Mr. Ellison, Mr. Zuckerberg, and Mr. Bloomberg.

But what is not socially useful is to call these or any other contributions "giving back." The implication of the term is that the donor has taken something from society by earning money and that this has created an obligation to return something through charity. This view of charity is very counterproductive and leads to the general demonization of markets, which has become rife in our society. The important point is that the act of creating wealth is itself productive. In a market economy, the only way to become wealthy is to create some good or service that others find valuable. The wealthy may contribute to social good by giving to charity, but before that, they created even more social good through the very behaviors that created their wealth.

However much good Mr. Gates may do through his foundation, the social benefits pale in comparison to his contribution through Microsoft and the computer revolution he helped to create. Mr. Gates was able to gather for himself only a small portion of these benefits; the rest went to all of us in the form of consumer surplus. Mr. Buffett is a highly skilled investor, which means that he created huge amounts of social wealth by contribution to the efficient allocation of capital. In an earlier era, John D. Rockefeller made his money by rationalizing the production and distribution of petroleum, first for kerosene lighting and then for automobiles. He then gave a lot of it to the Rockefeller Foundation.

Henry Ford (a vicious anti-Semite) nonetheless created huge amounts of social wealth (which also benefited Jews) by developing methods of producing automobiles at low cost. In fact, when Henry Ford "gave back," he did it in part by publishing an anti-Semitic newsletter, *The Dearborn Independent*, and contributing to other hateful causes. Hitler borrowed heavily from Ford's newspaper.

This illustrates that in producing wealth it is necessary to benefit people by satisfying their desires, but in giving back it is possible to do harm as well as good, depending on the targets of giving. For example, the Koch Brothers, George Soros, and Michael Bloomberg all give back by contributing large sums to political action, but it is impossible that they are all contributing to social good since the causes they advocate are diametrically opposed. (The Koch Brothers are strongly pro-market, while Mr. Soros is strongly anti-market, and Mr. Bloomberg is somewhere in between, though on the pro-regulation side.)

Giving to charity is often meritorious, but the benefits of charity are secondary to the benefits created by earning the wealth that can be contributed.

COOPERATION AND COMPETITION

Another reason why people may prefer socialism to capitalism is that we view capitalism as being competitive, and we tend to dislike competition. I have examined the usage of the word "competition" using Google. Here are some common modifiers of "competition" and the number of Google references to each: "cutthroat competition" (256,000), "excessive competition" (159,000), "destructive competition" (105,000), "ruthless competition" (102,000), "ferocious competition" (66,700), "vicious competition" (53,500), "unfettered competition" (37,000), "unrestrained competition" (34,500), "harmful competition" (18,000), and "dog-eat-dog competition" (15,000). Conversely, for "beneficial competition" there are 16,400 references. For "beneficial cooperation" there are 548,000 references and almost no references to any of the negative modifiers of cooperation. Thus, people have no difficulty in thinking of negative connotations of "competition" and are less inclined to think of competition than of cooperation as beneficial.

However, in fact capitalism is much more cooperative than is socialism. The fundamental unit of capitalism is the transaction, and a transaction is a cooperative act. In a transaction, both parties benefit.

There is competition in a capitalist economy, but the competition is for the right to cooperate. When Ford and Chevy compete for your business, they are competing for the right to transact with you—to cooperate with you. Whoever offers you the best deal will get the business. In fact, a market economy is the most cooperative entity in the world.

Think about a simple act—buying a shirt in a department store. Think about all the cooperative transactions that have occurred to make this possible. The cotton was grown somewhere else—maybe Egypt. The farmer needed fertilizer, seed, and pesticide to grow the crop. He also needed tractors, perhaps made in the U.S. from steel that was made in large factories. Someone had to build these factories from numerous inputs. That only gets us started—the cotton was shipped in ships made from steel, made somewhere, and sold in a department store. The department store employees had to eat, wear clothes, and get to work. Somewhere in that chain is someone who took an economics course from me at Emory, and so became more productive. I don't want to go on, but you can see that millions of people were involved in producing the shirt. All of them are cooperating, and all are driven by the profits they might make from the products and services they provide. The entire world economy is a huge web of cooperative interactions.

CHAPTER 16

CAPITALISM

I have discussed some aspects of capitalism to contrast it with socialism. However, a chapter setting forth the main points of capitalism will help you understand exactly how it differs from socialism.

Under capitalism the *only* (legal) way to make money is to provide some good or service to others that is valued. You must create value for others to earn an income in a capitalist society. The more value you create, the higher your income. This is a hugely important point. We saw that under socialism, government uses the threat of force to obtain resources, which it then distributes as it sees fit. This option is not available to anyone (except government) in a capitalist economy. Any firm or any person must perform some useful service or offer some useful good to earn any money. Even a monopoly must sell something to earn an income. So we may criticize monopolies, but a monopoly is better than not having the good at all.

Although a market economy is often called "competitive," it is actually cooperative. The most basic economic element is a transaction, which is a voluntary exchange between two parties. *Both* parties must agree to the terms of the transaction, and so both must benefit. It is in this sense that a market economy is cooperative.

Competition is important in a cooperative economy. When two firms compete, they are competing for the right to cooperate (transact with) with consumers. When two potential employees compete for the same job, they are competing for the right to work for (cooperate with) a firm.

Think of yourself, looking for a job. You are competing with the set of job seekers—perhaps ten, maybe even a hundred. But you are cooperating with millions of other people—all those who sell you products, all those who make the products, all those who make the inputs for those products, all those who work in your enterprise to produce the products you sell, and all those who buy your products. In a market economy you compete with a small set of people, but you cooperate with almost everyone else, directly or indirectly.

Here is an example: Walmart moves to town, and some businesses go bankrupt and shut down. People say, "Isn't it a shame that competition with Walmart has driven out all those businesses." But here is another way to views the same situation. "Isn't it great that Walmart has done a better job of cooperating with the people of the town to give them better choices at better prices?" Same story, but different views.

Although we call an economy competitive, it is really cooperative. Competition is important because it assures that cooperation takes place between the right agents and at the most favorable terms. But the work of the economy is done by cooperation. Cooperation is what generates the benefits of a market economy—the consumer surplus. Because we naturally think of competition as being "zero-sum" by calling an economy competitive, economists have created a negative view of the economy, but it is actually cooperative and positive-sum.

There is also competition in a socialist economy, but it is competition to deal with the bosses, not with the citizens. In a market economy, you do better if you can do a better job of cooperating with citizens and customers. In a socialist economy, you do a better job if you can better compete with those who have used force or the threat of force to extract money from those who have earned it. It is in this sense that a market economy is a bottom up economy, while a socialist economy is a top down economy.

People worry that income in a capitalist economy is too unequal, but a capitalist society generates more income than any other economy. As a result, the poor in a capitalist society are actually better off than the non-poor in many other societies. For example, per capita income in China is less than $10,000 per year. In the U.S., median income of the *lowest* 20 percent of the population is over $13,000. In other words, the poorest 20 percent of the population in the U.S. is richer than the average person in China.

Capitalism is actually a rather simple system. This is because it harnesses normal human motivations, especially the desire to better oneself. In a pure capitalist system, there is a minimal role for government. Government should enforce property rights against fraud and theft, and should itself forbear from arbitrarily taking property rights. Government should also enforce private contracts, provide defense against foreign enemies, and should in some circumstances provide for the public health, as we are seeing now. While most governments do many more things, some of which are useful, these are the basic points. This has been well known for a long time. If any government does not perform these functions and particularly forbear from arbitrary takings, it is because those running the government are interested in their own wealth and power, not in the welfare of the citizens.

There are a few basic principles of capitalism that are non-intuitive but do not require technical skills to understand. If these were more widely understood, then markets would be viewed more favorably, and socialism would lose its appeal. A very important distinction is the difference between the size of the pie—the amount of goods and services produced—and the division of the pie—who gets how much. Economics focuses on the size of the pie—how can society's scarce resources be used to produce the most efficient bundle of goods and services?

Voters often focus on the division of the pie—who gets how much? This is because untrained people often view the world as zero-sum. Indeed, zero-sum thinking is probably the cause of most errors in economic thinking, including a belief in socialism. Economies can grow, and it is possible for the rich to get richer at the same time that the poor get richer. The common homily, "The rich get richer and the poor get poorer" is neither certain nor sure; it is totally contrary to fact in a growing market economy.

A basic premise of economics is that hundreds of millions of people can interact with each other with no central direction and no coordination, and yet can reach a consistent outcome which itself has certain efficient properties. This is Adam Smith's famous "invisible hand." Because this is not widely understood, there are frequent calls for central direction and central planning, despite its massive failure in the Soviet Union, Venezuela, and wherever else it has been tried. Capitalism does not need and cannot use central control. Rather, one of the beauties of capitalism is that it is self-directing. The system of free prices, well-defined property rights, and self-interest creates an equilibrium.

Economists also understand that selfish behavior can nonetheless lead to desirable outcomes. The uncoordinated behavior can be motivated by selfish ends, and yet the outcome will generally be efficient. Motives do not matter; outcomes do. In some sense, we are all out to maximize our incomes, but the way to do this in a market economy is to provide something that others want to buy. Steve Jobs and Bill Gates became fantastically wealthy by creating the computer revolution, and their financial wealth was only a small part of the massive social wealth they created. In a socialist economy, the way to gain wealth is to gain power over others.

All important innovations occur in capitalist economies. Russians are often proud of their inventiveness, but a search of websites for Russian inventions indicates that almost all of them (some of which are probably misattributed anyway) occurred before 1918, the Russian revolution, when Russia became communist. Similarly, Israel is now a hugely inventive economy, but this occurred after the capitalist reforms in the 1960s.

CHAPTER 17

FINAL SUMMARY

Socialism is becoming increasingly popular in the U.S. This is a puzzle because socialism has failed whenever it has been tried and has led to much human misery. Socialism is consistent with primitive pre-scientific thought but not with modern understanding of an economy.

The purpose of this book is to explain the effects of socialism on your lives. First, socialism will reduce the rate of growth in the economy, and so reduce your lifetime earnings. If you are a young person reading this book, then socialism will mean that for forty or forty-five years, your incomes will be smaller each year under a socialist economy than they would be under a capitalist economy. If growth rates are reduced for a long time, then incomes will be much lower. Even if socialism only lasts a few years, the harm to the economy will mean that your lives will be worse than if we do not ever become socialist.

Second, socialism will lead to much reduced choice in the marketplace. For example, current proposals for

"Medicare for All" eliminate all competing forms of insurance. Socialism in general will reduce your choices in the same way.

Socialists worry about income inequality. Any efforts to greatly reduce inequality will lead to higher taxes and reduced risk taking, and so will reduce technological change in the economy. It is surprising that young people who rely on the products of capitalism—computers, mobile phones, music services, online games, car services— are nonetheless opposed to capitalism. We are on the cusp of many new technologies, based on 5G, virtual reality, artificial intelligence, and biotechnical research, and it would be sad to reduce resources devoted to research by increasing taxes and reducing incentives for research.

Socialism will also reduce your freedom. Higher taxes mean that you have less control over your spending. Governments can also reduce the selection of products available, as in the Medicare for All example. Free markets are the source of most of our freedom; government generally restricts freedom, and socialism increases the power of government.

Finally, whenever socialism has been tried, it has failed. Past examples include the Soviet Union, East Germany, and Cuba. The most recent example is Venezuela, which was once the richest country in Latin America and now is a total economic and human disaster. Some point to the Nordic countries as examples of successful "democratic socialism," but they are no longer socialist. Indeed, they used the democratic part of "democratic socialism" to eliminate the socialism part.

SOURCES AND FURTHER READING

Much of the discussion of capitalism is available in any introductory economics textbook. If you decide to buy one, I suggest you buy an old edition. The material needed for further understanding of this book has not changed, and old texts are much cheaper.

A good source on socialism, which I have relied on here, is Chapter 8 of the 2019 *Economic Report of the President*, published by the Council of Economic Advisers, available free on the internet with a Google search. You can't go wrong with Milton Friedman's two great books, *Capitalism and Freedom* (University of Chicago Press, 1962, 1982, 2002) and (with Rose Director Friedman) *Free to Choose* (Harcourt, 1980). A recent book which defends capitalism is Tyler Cowen's *Big Business: A Love Letter to an American Anti-Hero* (St. Martin's Press, 2019). For a discussion of why people dislike capitalism, see my book, *The Capitalism Paradox: How Cooperation Enables Free Market Competition* (Bombardier Books, 2019). For a more humorous view of the evils of socialism, see Robert Lawson and Benjamin Powell, *Socialism Sucks: Two Economists Drink Their Way*

Through The Unfree World (Regnery, 2019). For a discussion of the costs of socialism, see "The Unaffordable Candidate: Bernie Sanders's $97 trillion agenda would impose incomprehensible costs," Brian_Riedl, *City Journal*, October 15, 2019. For a classic and more philosophical discussion, see Joseph Schumpeter, *Capitalism Socialism, and Democracy* (Harper, original edition, 1942, Second edition, 1946, Third edition, 1950).

Please also see: "Economic Freedom of the World Annual Report," Fraser Institute.

ACKNOWLEDGMENTS

Thanks to David Bernstein of Bombardier Books and Michael Finch of the David Horowitz Freedom Center for working out the details of the joint publishing arrangement. Thanks to my friend and frequent co-author, Jim Kau, for reading the entire manuscript and providing many helpful comments. Finally, thanks to my wife, Martie Moss, who has always encouraged my work and has generally made my life much better.

ABOUT THE AUTHOR

Barbara Banks Photography

Paul H. Rubin is Emeritus Dobbs Professor of Economics at Emory University. He has also worked as an economic consultant in Washington D.C. and held several senior positions in the Reagan Administration, including Senior Economist at the Council of Economic Advisers. He has earned several honors, including President of the Southern Economic Association. Professor Rubin has published a dozen books, about one hundred articles in professional journals, and two dozen op-eds in the *Wall Street Journal*.